EDUCATION AND GREEK AMERICANS
Process and Prospects

EDUCATION
AND
GREEK AMERICANS
Process and Prospects

Edited by

SPYROS D. ORFANOS
Board of Cooperative Educational Services
Rockland County

HARRY J. PSOMIADES
Queens College and The Graduate School
The City University of New York

JOHN SPIRIDAKIS
St. John's University

ΡΕLLΑ
PELLA PUBLISHING COMPANY, INC.
NEW YORK, NY 10018
1987

This book was published for The Center for Byzantine and Modern Greek Studies, Queens College of the City University of New York, which bears full editorial responsibility for its contents.

Views expressed in this publication are those of the authors and do not necessarily reflect the views of the sponsoring institution.

MODERN GREEK RESEARCH SERIES, V, OCTOBER 1987

EDUCATION AND GREEK AMERICANS
Process and Prospects

© 1987 by The Center for Byzantine and Modern Greek Studies, Queens College of the City University of New York, Flushing, New York 11367.

Library of Congress Catalog Card Number 87-063452

ISBN 918618-36-3

Cover design: Anastasios D. Orfanos

PRINTED IN THE UNITED STATES OF AMERICA
BY
ATHENS PRINTING COMPANY
NEW YORK, NY 10018

To the children, parents,
and educators
we work for and with.

MODERN GREEK RESEARCH SERIES

The purpose of this monograph series is to promote and disseminate scholarly works on the history, institutions, and the culture of the Greek people. It is sponsored and edited by the Center for Byzantine and Modern Greek Studies, Queens College of the City University of New York (formally jointly with the Greek Seminar of the Center for Mediterranean Studies of the American University). This is the fifth publication within the framework on the Modern Greek Research Project —Harry J. Psomiades, Professor of Political Science, Queens College of the City University of New York, director.

BOOKS OF THIS SERIES

TABLE OF CONTENTS

PREFACE

The papers contained in this volume were presented at a conference sponsored by The City University of New York— Center for Byzantine and Modern Greek Studies, Queens College and Center for European Studies, The Graduate Center and The Greek American Behavioral Sciences Institute in co-operation with the Greek Ministry of Culture and Science, the Greek Orthodox Archdiocese-Department of Education, the Hellenic American Educators Association, and St. John's University, Bilingual-ESL Center at the auditorium of the Graduate Center, C.U.N.Y. on May 15-17, 1986.

We wish to thank the Consul General of Cyprus, the Honorable Platon Kyriakides for the use of the Cyprus House for the conference reception; Dean Solomon Goldstein for the use of the C.U.N.Y. Graduate Center conference facilities; and the Atlantic Bank of New York for its material and moral support for the conference. We are also grateful to the Greek Ministry of Culture and Science-Greeks Abroad Division, the Jewish and Ethnic Studies Project of Queens College, which is funded by the New York State Education Department in Albany, the AHEPA Educational Foundation, and the Atlantic Bank of New York for grants which made possible the publication of this volume.

Regretfully and for a variety of reasons, not all of the papers presented at the conference appear in this volume. We are indebted to all those who participated in the conference. A special note of thanks to Anne Petsas and the Hellenic American Educators Associatio nfor input into planning and for providing hospitality to all conference participants, and to Effie Lekas and her staff of the Queens College Center for Byzantine and Modern Greek Studies for administrative and secretarial support.

S.D.O.
H.J.P.
J.S.

Flushing, New York

9

INTRODUCTION:
EDUCATING GREEK AMERICANS

SPYROS D. ORFANOS, HARRY J. PSOMIADES
AND JOHN SPIRIDAKIS

There are three major reasons for an edited volume on education and Greek Americans. First, during the last five years in this country the arena of education has been subjected to review in a manner that it never has before. Second, the educational issues facing the Greek American community have not been addressed in any fashion approaching the systematic or scientific. Last, Greek American Studies need to move away from general analytical studies, not because there is anything wrong with this approach, but because focused investigations on particular institutions often shed more light on the dynamic forces necessary for a better understanding.

We are now well into the "second wave" of educational reform in the United States. While earlier reports (e.g. *A Nation at Risk*, 1983; *Action for Excellence*, 1983) highlighted significant problems, recent reports and studies have addressed specific issues such as, the teaching profession (Carnegie Forum, 1986), findings on basic skills (U.S. Department of Education, 1986), reading (National Academy of Education's Commission on Education and Public Policy, 1985), and history and literature (Ravitch & Finn, 1987). Calls for reform, of course, continue with recognition of the grave limitations of elementary schools (Bennett, 1986), teacher training programs (Weiss, 1987), liberal arts education (Bloom, 1987), and the Reagan administration's educational policies (Clark & Astuto, 1986).

Education has been seen by many as a salvation. It is currently being viewed as the only real remedy for problems such as, Aquired Immune Deficiency (AIDS), the technological war with Japan, and the low value we place on children and youth. This is quite a charge to a field that is by its very nature complex and slow to respond to substantive change. The word "education" has even become a political buzzword for Democrats and Republicans (Hechinger, 1987; Shribman, 1987). While one Greek son and presidential hopeful, Gov. Michael S. Dukakis calls for Federal support of educational research and development, another, New York University President John Brademas (1986), reminds us that such research is not an exhilarating and commanding subject for elected politicians.

Sarason (1983) has written that we have always viewed education as a means of personal, social, intellectual, and vocational salvation at the same time that we are prepotently set to blame the schools for social malfunctioning. It is not hard to sense this view in many Greek Americans who interact with educational settings in a direct or indirect way. The expectations of Greek Americans regarding their culture, in all its facets and complexities, are quite high. It is noteworthy that many educational theorists view the major goal of schooling as cultural transmission (Perkinson, 1979). We believe this volume provides an opportunity to view the educational issues confronting Greek Americans in the context of broader national developments.

Creating a knowledge base in education is risky business. The task becomes even more complicated when applied to a changing community of over one million Greek Americans (Moskos, 1982), with three out of four Greek Americans born in America (Psomiades, 1982), with increasing numbers of mixed marriages (Scourby, 1984), and with strong signs of ethnic revival in the third generation (Constantinou & Harvey, 1985). Still, the attempt must be made in light of the fact that most ethnic research has been on race (Black and White), or more recently, on Hispanic and Asian communities (Milner, 1983). In order to understand the education phenomena faced by the Greek American community, original and objective knowledge is necessary. The chapters that follow are, we hope, a step in the right direction.

Lastly, the field of Greek American Studies is in its infancy despite some powerful and pioneering efforts (Moskos, 1982). Yet, while social psychologist Kurt Lewin's dictum,

"Everything is related to everything else," is probably right, we cannot study everything at the same time. When studying application, even systems theorists and social ecologists have come to see the wisdom of manageable investigations (Plas, 1986). Plato and John Dewey wrote that education is a social affair, and rightly belongs in the spheres of the social and behavioral sciences. A closer look at the specific interactions of students, parents, schools, and policies will be an addition to our present understanding of the forces operating in and around the Greek American community.

Plan of the Book

This edited volume is divided into two parts: Part I covers social and public policy issues; and, Part II covers educational and psychological issues. The division is more one of convenience, for the topics overlap. Part I, Social and Public Policy Issues, begins with Harry C. Triandis' social psychological and cross-cultural frameworks for understanding values and educational prospects and balancing such. Chrysie C. Costantakos provides survey data on intergroup conflict. John Spiridakis reviews the sociopolitical aspects of bilingual education. Lastly, Harry J. Psomiades addresses the relationships of elites within the Greek American community and between those elites and the Greek state in light of education.

Part II, Educational and Psychological Issues, begins with an original study for the volume by James R. Campbell, Charlene Connoly, and Lawrence Svrcek on the influence of Greek American parents on their children. Mary Teresa Ryan and Evelyn P. Altenberg address the psycholinguistic processes of the Greek and English alphabets. Terry Tchaconas presents data on the Greek and English reading strategies of public school students. Undertaking a language dominance test, Aristotle Michopoulos presents psychometric data on its development. Mary P. Lefkarites describes a workshop on sex education and provides a model for family life development. Finally, Spyros D. Orfanos and Sam J. Tsemberis present their original study undertaken for the volume on the needs of Greek American day schools.

The topic of educating Greek Americans is not exhausted in this volume. Future research needs to examine children's special needs, public schools, adult education, administrative decision-making, varied geographical regions and numerous other aspects of the phenomena. The present research areas must continue to be explored. While research informs action, it tends not to be the major influencing factor on those participating in the educational process or the making of decisions. Still, it is a step forward. If in the pages of this volume, the reader finds that more questions are raised than answered, the effort has been a successful one.

REFERENCES

Bennett, W. J. (1986). *First lessons: A report on elementary education in America*. Washington, DC: U.S. Department of Education.

Bloom, A. (1987). *The closing of the American mind: How higher education has failed democracy and impoverished the souls of today's students*. New York: Simon & Shuster.

Brademas, J. (1986). *Washington, D.C. to Washington Square*. New York: Weidenfeld & Nicolson.

Carnegie Forum on Education and the Economy, Task Force on Teaching as a Profession. (1986). *A nation prepared: Teachers for the 21st century*. Washington, DC: Author.

Clark, D. L., & Astuto, T. A. (1986), The significance and permanence of changes in federal education policy. *Education Researcher, 15*, 4-13.

Constantinou, S. T., & Harvey, M. E. (1985). Dimensional structure and integenerational differences in ethnicity: The Greek Americans. *Sociology and Social Research, 69*, 234-254.

Education Commission of the States, Task Force on Education for Economic Growth. (1983). *Action for excellence: A comprehensive plan to improve our nation's schools*. Denver, CO: Author.

Hechinger, F. M. (1987, September 29). Presidential agendas. *The New York Times*, p. B7.

Milner, D. (1983). *Children and race* (2nd ed.). Harmondsworth: Penguin.

Moskos, C. C. (1982). Greek American Studies. In H. J. Psomiades & A. Scourby (Eds.), *The Greek American community in transition* (pp. 17-64). New York: Pella.

National Commission on Excellence in Education. (1983). *A nation at risk: The imperative for educational reform*. Washington, DC: U.S. Government Printing Office.

Perkinson, H. J. (1979, March). Learning from our mistakes. *Et Cetera*, 37-57.

Plas, J. M. (1986). *Systems psychology in the schools*. New York: Pergamon.

Psomiades, H. J. (1984). Contemporary Hellenism in the English-speaking world: Trends and prospects. In A. Farmakides, K. Kazazis,

N. M. Vaporis, A. Anagnostopoulos, and H. J. Psomiades (Eds.), *The teaching of Modern Greek in the English-speaking world* (pp. 8-12). Brookline, Mass.: Hellenic College.

Ravitch, D., & Finn, C. E. (1987). *What do your 17-year-olds know? A report on the first national assessment of history and literature.* New York: Harper & Row.

Sarason, S. B. (1983). *Schooling in America: Scapegoat and salvation.* New York: Free Press.

Scourby, A. (1984). *The Greek Americans.* Boston. Twayne.

Shribman, D. (1987, September 11). Education emerges as hot political issue, and the GOP seizes it. *The Wall Street Journal,* p. 1.

U.S. Department of Education. (1986). *What works: Research about teaching and learning.* Washington, DC: Author.

Weiss, S. (1987, October 5). Panel proposes CUNY abolish education major. *The New York Times,* p. B1.

Part 1

SOCIAL AND PUBLIC POLICY ISSUES

CHAPTER 2

EDUCATION OF GREEK AMERICANS FOR A PLURALISTIC SOCIETY

HARRY C. TRIANDIS

The focus of this paper is traditional Greek culture and how Greek Americans can best be educated so that they can function effectively in North America while retaining some of the desirable elements of their ethnic heritage.

In the first part of the paper I will present some of the key elements of traditional culture as they emerge from social science research. Then, I will comment on the desirability and undesirability of each element for effective functioning in North America, as well as for good mental health. Finally, I will examine how the education of Greek Americans may be structured in order to retain desirable elements and to suppress the undesirable ones.

This agenda requires a confrontation of cultural patterns and values. Thus, I believe it is essential that I make my values clear, so that you will be sensitized to my biases. It is impossible to discuss child-rearing and education without revealing one's biases. By telling you what my values are you can be aware of them.

First, my values are cosmopolitan and anti-ethnocentric. Most cultures are ethnocentric. That is, members of these cultures consider their own standards and values as the only correct ones. Other peoples' values and behaviors are judged according to how close they come to the values and behaviors of their own culture. Most cultures consider themselves to be at the center of the world. The Chinese called themselves the "central kingdom." The majority of the Amerindian tribes

use the name of the tribe to refer to "humans," thus implying
that those who are not members of the tribe are subhuman.
You know, of course, that the ancient Greeks called all those
who did not speak Greek "barbaroi," hence the English term
"barbarian"; they called all lands to their East the East, and
to their West the West, and that nomenclature is used in
English even today.

One can understand ethnocentrism as a process that en-
hances group identity, which has benefits for group survival.
In the past one could afford to be ethnocentric since wars had
limited consequences for the survival of mankind. Today the
situation is very different. Since the mid-20th century we live
on Spaceship Earth, and are able to eliminate all life on earth.
We must develop different skills for survival. Ethnocentrism
is now narrow, provincial, and dangerous to our survival. It
leads to cultural imperialism, prejudice and discrimination.
Thus, while it is healthy to be proud of our heritage, we must
also learn to tolerate different cultural patterns. We must learn
how to accommodate to cultural differences. All cultures have
elements that are both strengths and weaknesses. If we follow
the Socratic admonition to know ourselves we should also get
to know our weaknesses.

Second, my values favor mental health as well as physical
health. Good mental health means that people are able to face
their environment realistically, and to function effectively according to the requirements of that environment. They are
able to criticize and improve the environment, and also to
develop new cultural elements that creatively improve adjustment to their environment. In a very real sense, being Greek
American means that one is both Greek and American, but
also something more. It requires the creation of new cultural
elements that make adjustment to North America optimal.
There are elements of traditional Greek culture that simply
constitute burdens to a Greek American. There are elements
of American culture that are quite undesirable and lead to
high rates of delinquency, substance abuse, divorce, suicide,
and poor mental health. What we need is a synthesis that will
utilize those elements of traditional culture that can be helpful
in North America and avoid those elements of American culture that are undesirable.

The third value that I will mention today is achievement.
I think our main purpose here on earth is to make things a
little better for our fellow humans and the future generations.

This can be done if we create knowledge, wealth, services, and institutions that will make things better for others now and in the future. Obviously, this viewpoint is controversial, and many whose theological or political orientations differ from mine will utilize other priorities. My criticism of many current American practices stems from the excess of competitive individualism I see in this country, that often takes the forms of narcissism, of doing your own thing, of over-emphasis on achievement for self-glorification. There is a fine line between these two kinds of achievement. I think traditional Greek culture has employed a view of achievement that is much more healthy, and which can teach Americans a great deal.

With these preliminaries I will now turn to traditional Greek culture.

Traditional Greek Culture

There are many scholars who have studied traditional Greek culture from various perspectives (anthropological, sociological, psychological) and with diverse methodologies. The names that come to mind are Ernestine Friedl, John Peristianis, Popi Marinou Mohring, Vasso Vassiliou, Costantina Safilios-Rothschild, Dorothy Lee and Herbert Gans, but there are many others. I did some studies in collaboration with Vasso Vassiliou in the 1963-67 period. I am currently collaborating in some studies with James Georgas who is professor of social psychology at the University of Athens. There are numerous findings and I will select the most salient. I will concentrate on those aspects of traditional Greek culture that contrast most sharply with North American culture, because it is exactly where these discrepancies occur that the Greek American will find conflict, and uncertainty about how to behave.

Traditional Greek culture emphasizes ingroups and outgroups much more than North American culture. The definition of ingroup in Greece is "family and friends and other people potentially or obviously concerned with my welfare." Thus, in addition to family and friends, a guest who can potentially become a friend, or a physician or lawyer who has demonstrated true concern, become members of the ingroup. Those who are not in the ingroup are in the outgroup. That means, most people are outgroup.

The behavior of the traditional Greeks toward ingroup and outgroup members is sharply different. Toward ingroup members one is supposed to show not only trust, support, cooperation, but also self-sacrifice. There is an abundance of warmth and benevolence. Toward outgroup members one is suspicious, distrustful, and if there is an obvious opportunity, exploitative. If the outgroup member is not on guard, he is a "koroido," i.e., one can take advantage of that situation. After all, in the traditional Greek village, resources are very limited, and competition for them is high. The description of village life in the novel "Eleni" is fundamentally accurate. The petty jealousies of the village erupt into deathly confrontations, ultimately leading to her execution. Undoubtedly, this is an extreme case, but the novel does a good job of portraying the conflict between ingroup and outgroup.

Let me present to you some data that illustrate it in another context. Roy Feldman did a study of how people behave toward their own fellow nationals and toward strangers in Boston, Massachusetts, Paris, France and Athens, Greece. He used a number of different situations in which either a fellow national or a foreigner interacted with a sample of local people. He then recorded the response. I have time to talk about only one of these situations. In each city, he sampled 250 passerby in subway stations. The experimenter was either a native or a foreigner. In Athens it was either a Greek or an American. The experimenter stopped the passerby and asked for a simple favor: "Pardon me, Sir, would you post this letter for me?", then gave a plausible excuse for not doing it himself. The American spoke in broken Greek, but good enough to be understood. Feldman recorded the frequencies of the passerby agreeing to do the favor. Since the letter was addressed to him, he was able to check if, in fact, the passerby did mail it.

The prediction from our discussion of ingroups and outgroups is that Greeks will be more helpful to the American, who as a "xenos" is a potential ingroup member, than to a fellow Greek who is clearly an outgroup member. The data show that the percentage who helped the American was about the same as the percentage who helped in Boston or in Paris. Roughly 50% agreed to help in those cities, and there was no difference whether the request came from a fellow-citizen or a foreigner. However, in Athens, only 10% agreed to help a fellow Greek. So, this is consistent with my point that the behavior toward ingroup and outgroup is sharply different in

Greece, and not so different in the U.S. Greeks are impolite and suspicious toward outgroups.

An example will make it clear that people may switch their definition of whether you are ingroup or outgroup. When I go to Athens, I often call my old friends from high school. They usually have secretaries who answer the phone. The secretaries answer in a half-angry voice that contrasts rather dramatically with the sugary voice of American secretaries answering the phone. But, as soon as I identify myself, the Greek secretary becomes just as pleasant as the American.

The correct behavior within the ingroup is one of self-sacrifice. To put it differently, one bends backwards to see the other's point of view. The greatest virtue in Greece is being *philotimos*. That means doing what the ingroup expects you to do. One feels especially good about oneself by acting in a philotimos way.

Now, you might think that such behaviors are characteristically Greek. Certainly the vocabulary for describing them is Greek, but the behavioral pattern is culturally more widespread. The cultures of the Mediterranean, Latin America, and the Far East also have this pattern of sharply different behavior between ingroup and outgroup members. In an experiment conducted by one of my Chinese students from Hong Kong, he found that the way a person distributes resources differs when the recipient is an ingroup or an outgroup member. The subjects in this experiment played a game either with a friend or a stranger whom we will call "outgroup." During the game it was clear that the subject had contributed either twice as much or half as much as the outgroup member to the success of the game. The subject was then given $10 to divide with the partner. The point of the experiment was to see how the subject divided the money. When the experiment was done in Illinois, the subjects followed what we call the *equity* rule. That is, if they contributed twice as much to the success of the game, they gave themselves about $6.50 and their partners $3.50. When they contributed half as much as the partner to the success of the game they gave themselves about $4 and their partner $6. The Chinese subjects also used the equity rule when playing with a stranger. However, when they played with a friend they divided the money equally if they had made the greater contribution to the success of the game, and according to equity if the partner had made the greater contribution. In other words, if they had the upper hand with an ingroup member, instead of taking $6.50 they took about $5.25. That is obviously "bending backwards" behavior to make sure that the ingroup member does not feel cheated by the distribution.

When dealing with the ingroup one sees the relationship in a long-term time perspective. If you give a little more now, you will get it back when your friend does a favor for you some other time. But, if you are dealing with an outgroup member, fairness requires that you take notice of each member's current contributions.

This pattern of behavior, I suspect, is more general and is linked to a contrast between cultures that emphasize individualism where fairness and equity are very important values, and cultures that emphasize collectivism, or good relations within the ingroup, where equality and need are the salient bases of distribution. There is additional evidence that collectivist cultures pay more attention to need and tend to divide resources on the basis of equality, while individualist cultures use equity under all conditions. For example, if a businessman has some bonus to distribute, in individualistic cultures the competence of the employees is almost the only criterion for deciding how to distribute the money; in collectivist cultures need is given a much greater weight.

In collectivist cultures, behavior is regulated by ingroup-generated norms. How the ingroup is defined depends on the culture. It can be family, village, co-workers, fellow nationals, people who belong to the same tribe, religion, caste, etc. For different behaviors and in different situations these attributes will receive more or less weight. People do what is expected of them, according to norms generated by these ingroups. In individualistic cultures it is more acceptable to do one's own thing. If what one wants to do overlaps with what the ingroup wants done, that is fine, but if there is conflict the individual's goals are more important. This pattern of behavior is given legitimacy by emphasizing self-reliance, independence, freedom, and other values that are very important in individualistic cultures. Our research shows that in Greece self-reliance is also greatly valued, but only because it can lessen the burden of the ingroup. In individualistic cultures, such as the U.S., competition is also linked to self-reliance. In individualistic cultures the individual competes against other individuals; in collectivist cultures the ingroup competes against the outgroup. Now, this is psychologically significant.

If competition is defined in individual terms, failure means that the individual is defeated. The individual who has failed feels rejected, depressed, lonely; his self-esteem is at a low point. Suicide is not inconceivable. Substance abuse is often used as a means of escaping the depression. By seeking a high that drugs can provide, one can feel good about oneself again. By contrast, in collectivist culture, failure is the failure of the group. Of course, no one likes failure, but it is easier to take it if others share it. One can obtain emotional support from others; one can feel solidarity in defeat. Hope is more likely to exist when some of the members of the group express optimism about future successes. Thus, with social support, suicide is unlikely and substance abuse is rare.

The ingroups of individualists tend to be segmented and fluid, and there is little commitment to them. One may belong to scores of ingroups, but one's obligations toward each of them are very limited—e.g., meet once a week at 8 p.m. to play bridge. In collectivist cultures, the ingroups require much higher levels of commitment. Self-sacrifice (as when a brother will remain unmarried until all his sisters are married), inter-dependence, multiple types of support are constantly exchanged.

In the individualist cultures, if one does not get enough out of an ingroup; one simply drops it and gets another, or forms a new one. One sees people who are attached to their parents and people who see their parents rarely. Parent-child relations are seen as exchanges. If the child feels he is getting enough out of the relationship he sticks to it; if not, he drops it. Thus innumerable volunteer organizations and social support groups, from Alcoholics Anonymous to zoology clubs, carry on functions that in collectivist cultures are carried out by ingroups such as the family. Since the family does not have many functions in individualist cultures, there is less commitment to it.

These comments might suggest that a return to tradition collectivist patterns is desirable. But, let us not jump to such conclusions. There are substantial disadvantages to the collectivist cultural pattern. Essentially, the ingroup-outgroup distrust and conflict means that cooperation with outsiders is much less easy. Large organizations, such as corporations and political systems, require easy association of diverse individuals in terms of roles and functions, rather than behavior in personal terms. The traditional Greek pattern is superb for small restaurants, and other small-scale social systems, but when it is applied to larger social systems, it deteriorates to excessive conflict and non-cooperation, to distrust and to undermining of the work of others. In Greek politics, for example, the other political parties are outgroups, and people often think that it is better to defeat them than to collaborate with them. If the other party has a good idea that will really help the country, then it is particularly important to defeat it, since the other party will then gain the upper hand. So, we observe the political scene in the U.S., where there is a bipartisan foreign policy or defense policy, running more smoothly than in Greece where the political parties see a great abyss between their own position and that of the opposition.

Similarly, in large corporations in Greece, there is little communication and cooperation among units. There is almost built-in competition between units of the organization, with much infighting, undermining, and behind the scenes maneuvering, in order to put the other unit down, and thus glorify one's own.

Foa and Foa have presented a typology of exchanges of resources. According to their analysis, there are 6 resources that humans exchange: *love, services* and *status* are particularistic resources, because they are directed at particular others. *Information, money* and *goods* are universalistic resources, because they are exchanged without concern for who the other is. For example, those who broadcast in the mass media or sell in the stock market usually have little interest in which particular individual will tune in to hear the program, or will buy the stock.

Traditional societies are better in exchanging particularistic than universalistic resources. But, in dealing with political systems one mainly exchanges information, thus to exchange it particularistically is a mistake. In other words, we need to train people from collectivist cultures to exchange universalistic resources as people in individualistic cultures do.

It turns out, however, that the individualists have much to learn from the collectivists. It is the collectivists who are better in dealing with particularistic resources. For example, too many American parents, when they deal with their children, use money, a universalistic resource, instead of service, a particularistic resource. So, you see these rich, lonely kids, who have plenty of money to buy drugs, but do not have the services of their parents. As the society moves to a faster and faster pace, this phenomenon becomes even clearer. You can exchange money in seconds, by writing a check. You can not make love in seconds. So, more and more in modern cultures we exchange universalistic resources, because that does not take much time, and we try to substitute universalistic resources in situations that really require particularistic resources. Our kids need love, not so much money; they need our services, not exposure to hours of television; they need status, not more toys to play with.

However, traditional Greeks dealing with modern institutions also have problems. They try to use particularistic patterns of resource exchange in situations that call for universalistic exchanges. They deal with government bureaucrats, for instance, as if they were their relatives: "Won't you make an exception for *me*?"

In individualistic cultures exchanges tend to be regulated by tacit contracts. If you do this, I will do that. The idea is to be fair, so what you give me is worth as much to me, as what I give is worth to you. If I feel that I get more from you than it costs me to put up with you, then I stick to the relationship. If I feel I am not getting enough out of it, I drop you.

In collectivist cultures, relationships are regulated by norms, duties, and obligations. A person who is *philotimos* sticks to the obligations, even when it hurts a lot. One may complain, but one does not break the relationship. However, occasionally the relationship is broken. When the daughter loses her honor, or the brothers fight over property, relationships do break, and that tends to be cataclysmic. Just as there is a stronger commitment to the ingroup, so when there is a break it *really* hurts far more in collectivist cultures than in individualist ones.

These points have implications for the larger divorce rates we observe in individualistic cultures. The collectivist cultures have an advantage in the area of family stability. Fortunately, in North America, we can have our cake and eat it too. We can engage in universalistic exchanges with institutions such as the political system that require them, and we can marry other collectivists, and preserve family stability.

The strengths of the traditional Greek family are especially clear in the area of child rearing. The "philotimoi" parents give much of themselves to the children, not least of all *time*. That means good supervision of activities, less delinquency.

But also, less loneliness. Loneliness is the disease of the individualist cultures. Doing your own thing has consequences. Quite frequently, no one else wants to do that same thing. Loneliness is a much greater problem in the U.S. than in other cultures. Loneliness is mentioned spontaneously in free associations that Americans give while it is not mentioned in collectivist cultures. Teenage suicide is reaching an epidemic in the U.S. It is three times as high now as it was 25 years ago.

Another aspect of traditional Greek culture is *uncertainty avoidance*. This attribute is linked to generalized anxiety that something disastrous may happen. Greek parents worry much more than parents in individualistic cultures. These worries are unnecessarily exaggerated, but on the whole they have the effect of protecting their children from harm. However, Greek mothers overprotect, and Greeks overemphasize security—in jobs, in investments. This is not desirable when it comes to situations where moderate risks are desirable. In contrast to this Greek attribute, North Americans are likely to act adventurously. Shooting rapids is not a popular sport among Greeks, but there are many North Americans who like it. Few Greeks are famous car racers or tight-rope walkers, and none as yet has been on the top of Mt. Everest. In fact, people who do such things are often defined in Greek traditional culture as *trelloi*. A traditional Greek will take great chances to protect the ingroup, to fight in war, even to improve the finances of the ingroup with a risky investment, but sees no point in climbing Mt. Everest.

Sex differentiation is stronger and clearer in traditional Greece than in North America. This is an area where there is likely to be much conflict between traditional and acculturated Greek Americans, which can cause serious marital difficulties. In traditional Greek culture the men do the *important* things—the fighting, keeping the honor of the ingroup—and the women do the *essential* things—the raising of children, the preparation of the food, the shopping and paying of the bills. Much of the undesirable work is done by the women. Again, this is not uniquely Greek. Japan is very similar. One can see this cultural pattern as related to the importance of the ingroup. If the ingroup, rather than the person, is the unit of analysis, then differentiation by sex makes sense, since it allows the man free time to achieve for the ingroup. Spending time at the local *caffeneion*, the Greek is informed, able to make better political and economic decisions that will theoretically help the ingroup, and thus the wife. The wife by sacrificing herself makes this possible. Of course, from a North American perspective, this is male chauvinism.

Achievement in traditional Greece is not for the self-glorification of the individual, but for the ingroup. Parents are proud of their children's every success. They feel personally involved with the solution of a particular geometry problem that their child is facing in high school, while American parents keep a distance from such concerns. When success occurs, the whole ingroup celebrates. The person becomes even more integrated into the ingroup as a result of success. Achievement validates the ingroup, makes it worthy of admiration. Thus the identification of modern Greeks with the achievements of ancient Greeks is part of a natural pattern that one sees in many collectivist cultures. However, again, the battle of ingroups and outgroups must be recalled. The achievement of the ingroup is to be glorified, but the achievement of an outgroup member must be ignored. Since most Greeks that are not ingroup members are outgroup members, this explains the hostility of Greeks toward the achievements of their fellow Greeks.

A true story will illustrate my point: A Greek ministry needed an expert on de-salinization. So they wrote to M.I.T. and asked for the name of such an expert. M.I.T. wrote back, and gave them the name of the world's expert on the subject, who happened to be Greek. The ministry did not like that. They wrote back: "We asked for the name of an expert, not a Greek!"

Another theme is that in traditional Greece self-indulgence is a negative value. This fits well with the notion of collectivism. The person who is self-indulgent will perhaps not do his duties.

Greeks have a very high self-esteem. This has excellent functions. It is difficult to put them down. They do not feel discriminated by other groups. Failure does not mean too much. But, it has also an undesirable feature: we cannot take criticism. Criticize a Greek and you make an enemy. So, there are many situations where we cannot learn from our mistakes, because we are not told very clearly what these mistakes really are. It has also the problem that we are perceived by Americans as arrogant, dogmatic, all-knowing.

Let me mention some of the studies of stereotypes that Americans hold of Greeks and Greeks hold of Americans.

They do illuminate the relationship. Americans who live in Greece see Greeks as *inefficient, competitive, suspicious, emotional* and *rigid.* However, they also see them as *charming, witty, obliging,* and *honest.* To interpret these results we must remember that the relationship between an American and the Greeks he meets is likely to be either ingroup or outgroup, and that the quality of the social behavior will be quite different depending on how the relationship is defined. If it is ingroup, then *charming, witty, obliging* and *honest* are perfectly descriptive; if it is outgroup, *competitive, suspicious* and *rigid* fit. Since Americans value time much more than Greeks, some of the behavior they observe is likely to be seen by them as *inefficient.* Since Greeks feel it is important to express and not suppress emotions, much of Greek behavior does appear *emotional.*

On the other hand, Greeks perceive Americans in Greece as *efficient,* but *cold, arrogant, suspicious, dull, competitive* and *sly.* Again, it depends on the ingroup or outgroup definition. If the American is ingroup, then his high evaluation of time is likely to lead to *efficient.* But if he is outgroup, the other attributes follow.

The cultural differences outlined above have implications for interpersonal relationships. Greeks expect social behavior to be more personalized, intimate, and warm with ingroup members, and more distant with outgroup members. Thus, when they first interact with an American, they are likely to test the ingroup/outgroup status of the relationship. Americans act in a very friendly, open way when they meet new people, but draw a very definite line very soon after. A constant complaint from foreign students in the U.S. is that they start relationships with Americans and these relationships go nowhere. The Americans are unwilling to make these relationships intimate. The same process can be seen with Greeks. They start the relationship warmly, and it looks like it might be an ingroup relationship so they start asking personal questions, such as "How much do you make per month?" "How much did you pay for your shirt?" The American withdraws in response to these questions. The Greek interprets this withdrawal as outgroup behavior, so he starts emitting outgroup behavior, and so what looked first like a good relationship turns sour.

The problem, of course, is the misinterpretation of the meaning of behavior. We all make attributions, that is, assign causes to the social behaviors we observe. These attributions provide meaning to the behavior. So, when the Greek asks, "How much do you make?", he is indulging his curiosity, but he is also saying: "We are ingroup, so you can tell me." The American sees it as an intrusion, as a means to constrain him from doing his own thing. He withdraws, and thus, again we have misattributions. The Greek does not see the American's unwillingness to reveal his income as unwillingness to discuss a taboo subject, which it is, but as cold rejection—the kind of behavior one expects of outgroup members.

We have developed training procedures that explain such attributions to Americans, so that they will not get into the trap of misunderstanding Greek behavior. Similar training could be developed in the other direction, for Greeks interacting with Americans, and might be helpful to newcomers.

Evaluation of Cultural Traits

Collectivism is both desirable and undesirable, depending on the criteria used. From the point of mental health, collectivism has much to recommend itself. Consider undesirable life events, such as getting fired from a job, or loss of a loved one. Being integrated into ingroups and receiving social support reduces stress, and high stress is related to many physical and mental illnesses. Also, where achievement can be facilitated by the ingroup, collectivism has advantages.

However, in political life, and in situations where achievement requires cutting oneself off from the ingroup, as well as in large organizations, collectivism can be counterproductive.

So, the typical collectivist is less lonely, anomic, and alienated than the typical individualist; extreme individualism is linked to high rates of divorce, suicide, delinquency, crime, and poor mental health. On the other hand, the typical collectivist tends to be more ethnocentric, with his or her ingroup as the center of the universe, and the corresponding ethnic group surrounding it. As a result, there is less appreciation of the good qualities of outgroups. The large differences seen between ingroups and outgroups lead to more conflict, and more dogmatic thinking. Furthermore, while the collectivist is loyal to the ingroup, there is the danger that the ingroup will take advantage of it, and eliminate individuality, creativity, and originality. Sometimes self-sacrifice is undesirable from the point of view of both giver and receiver of the benefits. Thus, training people to be self-reliant and independent, so they can escape the pressures of ingroups, has some merit. At the same time, keeping the ingroup as a source of inspiration, support, and as an audience that applauds one's accomplishments, is very valuable for good mental health.

So there is a delicate balance between ingroup support and inspiration, and ingroup exploitation of the individual. On the whole, Greeks have been very successful in balancing these forces, and perhaps the admonition contained in *pan metron ariston* has much to do with that. One must note that there are collectivist ingroups in Africa and Latin America that prevent individuals from developing their full potential, and that hinders economic development.

On the other hand, there is a need for Greeks to improve the way they deal with political and large organizational systems, and learn to utilize universalistic resources as they are meant to be utilized and not particularistically. Learning to respect human rights and cultural as well as political diversity has at times been difficult in Greece, with the worst recent period occurring in 1967-74. Fortunately, there has been much improvement in recent years.

Uncertainty avoidance is a desirable attribute. The anxiety behind it leads to hard work, and Greeks are superb workers, only matched by the Japanese. Hard work is an escape from anxiety. There are studies showing that the countries that are high on this attribute have had the most dramatic increases in GNP in the recent quarter century. However, uncertainty avoidance is also related to overprotectiveness that parents show toward their children, which sometimes reduces self-reliance. Given that self-reliance is such a high value in North America, a Greek-American who is not self-reliant is likely to have a hard time in this culture. On the other hand, North Americans overdo the self-reliance-independence bit and leave their children insecure and sometimes unable to deal with the fierce personal competition of this culture, particularly when they do not receive ingroup emotional support. Again, a delicate balance must be struck between two extremes. Greek child-rearing is high in both warmth and control of the child; American child-rearing is moderate in warmth and high in autonomy. Probably the ideal for Greek Americans is to retain the warmth of the Greek pattern, and to strike a point intermediate between the extreme autonomy and extreme control patterns.

Of course, there are also differences between the way boys and girls are raised by parents. In both cultures boys are given more autonomy than girls. Perhaps the optimal point is for Greek Americans to give as much autonomy to their girls as Greeks give to their boys, and as much autonomy to their boys as mainstream Americans give to their girls.

Sex differentiation can be desirable under some conditions. For instance, in collectivist cultures, achievement is group rather than individual achievement, and in that case specialization of function along gender lines can increase the probability of group achievement. Make no mistake. The phenomenal success of small Greek enterprises in North America would not have been possible if the women had not worked as hard as the men. At the same time, we must recognize that as a family experiences upward mobility, with some of its members becoming professionals, the definition of achievement in ingroup terms becomes difficult. Certainly, as members of the family join large organizations, it is difficult to use the old definition of achievement. Furthermore, from the point of mental health, large sex differentiation is undesirable because it puts down women and reduces their self-esteem. So, what is functional when the ingroup is the unit of achievement is not functional in modern society. Sex differentiation, as found in traditional Greece, is male chauvinism in North America. Thus, a de-emphasis on sex differentiation is needed, particularly as the family becomes socially/upwardly mobile.

Education of Greek Americans

I turn now to my last topic. Clearly there are attributes of traditional Greek culture we want to preserve and some we want to suppress. The warm support of the ingroup we want to treasure; the putting down of the outgroup we want to suppress. The interdependence, the self-sacrifice we want to keep; the tyranny of the ingroup we want to eliminate. Ingroups are fine, as long as they do not prevent self-realization. The hard work we want to keep; the extreme concern and worry that results in overprotection and too much control over the individual we want to suppress. Sex differentiation we want to reduce, and as the family moves to definitions of achievement that are individual we want to eliminate it.

In all these recommendations, we need to keep in mind the moderating effects of social status and modernity. The traditional culture is functional when the family is in a traditional or a lower socioeconomic environment; it becomes less functional as the family operates in modern environments. But, let us guard against making all Greek Americans carbon copies of mainstream Americans. We want to preserve their Greekness in as many aspects as we can, particularly in family life.

Thus, when parents emphasize ingroup/outgroup distinctions, the us vs. them differences, one is creating people who can function well under collectivism. When the rewards are given to the group rather than to the individual, one also moves toward collectivism. When obedience and *philotimo* are stressed one moves toward collectivism. Moving toward collectivism is desirable, particularly for mental health, divorce, suicide, substance abuse, etc. But one must not overdo it. Giving the child a chance to relate to various groups, as happens when the child is sent to live abroad, or in any case away from home, or when education is designed to include diverse elements about other peoples' values, religions, cultures, political and economic systems, etc. the young people are prepared for life in a pluralistic society.

Let us design the educational systems for Greek Americans to preserve interdependence, to keep some rewards at the ingroup level, but also to increase the appreciation of outgroups. Let us continue our emphasis on hard work, but let us reduce our emphasis on sex differentiation.

Conclusion

I have outlined some elements of traditional Greek culture that are desirable and undesirable, and have commented on traditions and techniques that can maintain and suppress them. The exact balance is difficult to achieve, and will change with circumstances. We need to design educational systems that allow balance in the emphasis of various elements.

Πᾶν μέτρον ἄριστον.

CHAPTER 3

THE GREEK AMERICAN
SUBCOMMUNITY:
INTERGROUP CONFLICT

CHRYSIE M. COSTANTAKOS*

Diversity in the definition of ethnic identity within the Greek ethnic community has an impact on its organizational structure, including the educational prospects of survival and transmission of Greek heritage. The community subgroupings under consideration in this paper are the foreign-born groups, the old and recent migrants, and the native-born groups of the second and third generation Greek Americans.

Ethnicity is a powerful instrument in determining identity, the points of reference which define our relations to others, both as individuals and as groups. Ethnicity constitutes a sense of commonality transmitted over generations by the family and reinforced by the surrounding community. It is more than national origin, religion or race. It involves conscious and unconscious processes that fulfill deep psychological needs. They are psychological needs for identity, belongingness, security, self-esteem, and a sense of historical continuity. It is the group bonding of a shared fate, a shared symbolic and basic value system. Indeed, one may think of the bonding of a group as the prerequisite of the survival and evolution of culture. It is thus, the sense of commonality, the shared culture which is critical for values, attitudes, perceptions, modes of expression, behavior and identity. The concept of ethnicity is multidimensional and complex.

*The author wishes to thank Sam Tsemberis for his invaluable assistance in analyzing the data and commenting on an earlier draft.

As Lopata (1976) points out, "part of the problem in studying ethnicity is the complexity of sources from which people can draw ethnic identities" (p. 115). "How ethnic does a person have to be to be called an ethnic? Which traits of national culture or ethnic style of life does a person have to exhibit? How influential must such an identity be in the behavior of the person, in self-feelings, in the behavior of other members of the same ethnic group and of outsiders, toward him or her, before it is clearly identifiable?" (p. 111). Is ethnic identification to be defined as a matter of degree and the preference by generation for things ethnic over things American? (Kitano, 1969). Is ethnicity to be defined in a sense of an ingroup/outgroup dichotomy and a subjective culture specificity?

The difficulty of defining boundaries of ethnic identification, self and other-imposed labeling, often stems from the oversimplication of the content of ethnicity which overlooks the different identity packages, the subtypologies which constitute the broader and more complex ethnic identity. Definitions for the most part ignore the evolution of culture, the modification of the content and its multifaceted components which range between dimension of old traditional folk culture and present day culture of social change and modernity.

They ignore that milieu change, complexity and social change impose changes in the prevailing value systems and operating value orientations. In the case of the Greeks of diaspora, moving to the complex milieu of an industrialized, urbanized society necessitated that the social conduct associated with Greekness, the Greek core-culture, could no longer be regulated by ingroup norms which in Greek traditional culture constituted the all important social institution. While in Greek core-culture(the traditional milieu), a Greek's perceptions and judgment were strongly influenced by the prevailing norms of the community, the ingroup interdependence, such norms could not very well be operational in the New World. These ingroup norms became less and less functional in the new environment, roles becoming more important than norms with the social milieu allowing for more individualized interpretation of the social context and a more individualized definition of Greekness (Triandis, 1972, Vasiliou & Vasiliou, 1973). Anyone who is looking for a definition of what constitutes ethnicity for the Greek American, writes Scourby (1980), cannot expect a clear, simple definition. "Ethnic identity is extremely difficult to pinpoint. The concept is a fluid one and changes along a continuum of such variables as generation, education, occupation and class . . . so much of ethnic identity is an unconscious experience as well as an ambivalent experience." (pp. 43, 50).

Accounts of migration experiences and assimilation observe that the processes involve, unrest, conflict, and hostility. (Fitzpatrick, 1971; Fong, 1973; Weiss, 1970). Intergenerational differences in rates of acculturation generate conflict, antagonistic perceptions and at times disruption of life in ethnic communities. Subgroupings experience conflict and stress produced by acculturation gaps, the greatest stress experienced by those whose levels of acculturation are most discrepant in self, family and ethnic identity perceptions. "Stress is especially pronounced in relations between generations because of the varying degrees in which traditional value orientations are abandoned and American ones are adopted." (Papajohn & Spiegel, 1975, p. 270).

Thus, ethnicity is in a perpetual state of evolution as it adapts, absorbs, borrows, and rejects aspects of cultures in contact. In a world of transitions there is conflict generated as old roles are undone and new ones emerge. Any change in the boundaries of one social role can potentially affect the whole interlocking system of role relationships (Fong, 1973). Ethnic subcommunities sift through varieties of input, conflicting value systems, social roles, foreign models, and demands of new environments. It is the assumption underlying the reported investigations that the evidence of intergroup conflict within the Greek American subcommunity, comprised of a diverse constituency of old migrants, recent migrants and native-born generations is indeed due to the diversity of perceptions of what constitutes Greekness, the existence of subtypologies within the ethnic community, the inevitability of an acculturation gap, and marginality in relation to the Greek American community, the American culture and modern Greece. The subgroupings of the Greek American subcommunity operate from different frames of reference, addressing a new brand of Hellenism in America, a brand which runs between the polarities of Hellenism and Americanism, an American Hellenism, you might say. The subgroupings hold stereotypic views of each other, experiencing antagonism, and the stress of all those who hold marginal positions. They perceive their social environment with the specificity of their subjective culture. It is therefore reality as perceived with significant across-milieu variations (Triandis, 1972, Vasiliou & Vasiliou, 1973).

The Studies

In an attempt to gain deeper insight into the intergroup conflict of the ethnic subcommunity, two exploratory studies were undertaken. In an earlier study, the results of which have been partly reported (Costantakos, 1980) a total of 50 in-depth interviews were conducted. To this sample were added ten interviews, using the same data collection instrument and conducted independently during the time frame of the second study. The sample included old migrants, recent migrants, second and third generation native-born Greek Americans. An interview guide consisting of sixty-six open-ended statements was the instrument of data collection. Open-ended questions assure flexibility of response and extend the benefits of non-verbal communication clues. They are especially useful for exploratory studies aimed at generation of theory, that is "generation hypothesis' rather than "hypothesis testing." (Glaser and Strauss, 1967). The statements reflected attitudinal and behavioral components along lines of ethnic identification, perceptions of sex roles, sources of identification, such as ethnicity in its classic and modern manifestations: tradition, language, church, family, and kin. Many of the interviews extended for as long as three to four hours and included questions referring to processes of continuity such as contact with the old country, the effect of continuous migration, church and community participation, marriage within and outside the group, family and kin interaction. The interview guide was translated into Greek and use was made of the Greek language when necessitated in the case of migrant respondents.

The second study presently undertaken sought to more precisely identify the characteristics the subgroupings attribute to each other within the framework of an ethnic identification continuum which runs the polarities of Greekness and Americanism. One part of the study explored traits best and least liked for each subgrouping within the foreign and native-born groups, in a sense the characteristics attached to each of the labels, Greek, Greek American, American Greek,

American. Another part addressed group variances based on a weighted scale of psychological attributes. The questionnaire included fifty-six questions and was comprised of demographic, behavioral, attitudinal data as well as some specific socio-psychological dimensions. The questionnaire was in English and no need was presented for translation. The first part consisted of demographic data such as age, sex, generational status, level of education, and other census information. The second part dealt with psycho-social attributes, the perceptions the subgroupings hold of each other.

Perception is used in its basic meaning to denote the awareness of one's environment obtained through interpreting sense data, direct or intuitive cognition, mental images interpreted in the light of experiences, and milieu specificity. People may carve out different perceptual experiences from the same scene or event as they select the world differently and view it through their own individual lenses. The data are derived from 102 questionnaire responses. The sample was drawn from both secular and religious organizations and was fixed by circumstance. The bulk of the questionnaires were responded to by students of Greek descent at Queens College of the City University of New York and through the courtesy of the Center of Byzantine and Modern Greek Studies. Table II gives the description of the characteristics of this sample.

Methodological limitations for both studies are acknowledged in view of the inherent weaknesses of the data collection instruments. There is no claim that the samples chosen represent the whole or of the ability to say with any degree of accuracy whether information supplied by the sample is certainly true or not true about the universe from which the samples were drawn. Interpretations and inferences, therefore, will have to be evaluated within the context of such limitations. At no point is randomness claimed in the selection process and the data are to be considered only as applicable to the groups of the studies and regarded as suggestive and tentative.

Additional limitations pertain to the second study and the lack of consistency of the number of items responded to by the sample as a number of respondents did not answer all of the items of the questionnaire. Of particular interest was the avoidance of responding to open-ended statements eliciting the best and least liked characteristics of the subgroupings. While descriptions were uninhibited in the interviews, when question items attempted to close in on specific attributes, the respondents found it difficult to be pinned down, thus possibly reflecting a dichotomy of cognitive and emotional levels. A number of foreign-born respondents failed to answer the items eliciting descriptions of best and least liked attributes. One can speculate on reasons which might include classroom time limitations and/or language barriers. It is also possible that the problem reflected a hesitation stemming from the vagueness of the ethnic identification concept. As there was no representation of old migrants to speak of, it was not possible to delve into the distinctions between the old migrants and the recent migrants projected in the earlier study of interviews.

Description of the Sample of the First Study

The age of the sixty interviewees ranged from the late twenties to seventies. The majority of respondents fell into the age brackets of late teens and twenties. They were followed by the groups of fifty to sixty and thirty to forty in a descending order. Fifty-two per cent of the interviewees were male and 48 per cent female. Fifty-seven per cent were born in the United States, 42 per cent in Greece, and 2 per cent in previously Greek territories or territories with substantial Greek populations. Sixty-three per cent originated from urban centers and 37 per cent from rural areas. Fifty-seven per cent had their schooling in the United States, 22 per cent in Greece, and 22 per cent had educational exposure in both countries. This was a rather highly schooled group, 25 per cent had some college education and 35 per cent were college graduates with some post-graduate schooling or professional training. Fifteen per cent had grammar school education. The rest had some high school education or were high school graduates. Sixty-seven per cent reported good to fluent Greek language proficiency and 70 per cent good to fluent proficiency in the English language. Two per cent spoke no English and 10 per cent gave their proficiency in English as poor.

Occupationally, 42 per cent fell into the professional and managerial categories and 20 per cent were students. The rest were housewives, clerical and kindred workers and craftsmen. Only 5 per cent were unskilled, operative service workers. The group was split with regard to marital status, 47 per cent were married, and 45 per cent were single. Of those married, 38 per cent had married within the group, and 17 per cent out of the group, reflecting endogamy on a higher level than reported for the Greek American community at large. Generationally, 15 per cent of the sample were early migrants, having migrated before 1940. Another 27 per cent of migrants had migrated more recently, the majority in the sixties and seventies. Fifty-two per cent were members of the Church, and 42 per cent were active. Forty-three per cent were members of community organizations but only 33 per cent reported active involvement. Twenty-three per cent were active in the past but no longer. See Table 1.

TABLE 1
DEMOGRAPHIC AND DESCRIPTIVE VARIABLES FOR THE FIRST STUDY
N = 60

Demographic Variables		*N*	%
Age	10-20	13	21.7
	20-30	20	30.3
	30-40	9	15.0
	40-50	7	11.7
	50-60	4	6.7
	60-70	3	5.0
	70-80	4	6.7
Sex	Male	31	51.6
	Female	29	48.3
Place of birth	U.S.A.	34	56.6
	Greece	25	41.7
	Other	1	1.5
Location (Urban vs. rural)	Urban	38	63.3
	Rural	22	36.6
Educational background	U.S.A.	34	56.7
	Greece	13	21.7
	Both	13	21.7
Educational level	Grammar School	9	15.0
	Some high school	5	8.3
	High school graduate	10	16.7
	Some College	15	25.0
	College graduate or higher	21	35.0

TABLE 1 (continued)
DEMOGRAPHIC AND DESCRIPTIVE VARIABLES FOR THE FIRST STUDY
$N = 60$

Other Descriptive Variables		N	%
Greek language proficiency (Overall evaluation by respondent)	None	2	3.3
	Poor	8	13.3
	Fair	10	16.7
	Good	26	43.3
	Fluent	14	23.3
English language proficiency	None	1	1.7
	Poor	6	10.0
	Fair	5	8.3
	Good	15	25.0
	Fluent	33	55.0
Occupation	Professional	20	33.3
	M.O.P. (Managers. officials, proprietors)	5	8.3
	Clerical and kindered workers, sales workers	6	10.0
	Small shopkeepers	0	0.0
	Craftsmen, foremen and kindered workers	4	6.7
	Unskilled, operative service workers	3	5.0
	Students	12	20.0
	Housewives	5	8.3
	None (retired)	5	8.3
Marital status	Single	27	45.0
	Married	28	46.7
	Separated	0	0.0
	Divorced	2	3.3
	Widowed	3	5.0
Intermarriage[a]	Yes	10	16.7
	No	23	38.3

[a] $N = 33$.

TABLE 1 (continued)
DEMOGRAPHIC AND DESCRIPTIVE VARIABLES FOR THE FIRST STUDY
$N = 60$

Other Descriptive Characteristics		N	%
Personal generational status	First generation (Old migrants)	9	15.0
	First generation (Recent migrants)	16	26.7
	Second generation	20	33.3
	Third generation	10	16.7
	Second and third (intergenerational)	3	5.0
	Children of intermarriages	1	1.5
	Other	1	1.5
Church membership	Yes	31	51.7
	No	29	48.3
Church activity	Active	25	41.7
	Inactive	29	48.3
	Active in the past	6	10.0
Membership in community organizations	Yes	26	43.3
	No	34	56.7
Organizational Activity	Active	20	33.3
	Inactive	26	43.3
	Active in the past	14	23.3

Findings of the First Study (N = 60)

Responses to the questions and statements of the interview guide were analyzed comparing foreign-born and native-born groupings. The findings are based on case study analysis, a tool which is most useful in that it provides for a realistic portrayal of attitudes, values and role behaviors, and allows for insights and opportunity to draw inferences. For the most part, responses of this study reflected strong intergroup conflict, each group holding its own views of the other. Quotations ranged from violent criticism to benign acceptance. As an example, speaking on the subject of the recent migrant, old migrants and second generation respondents remarked:

> Most male Greek Americans do not get along with Greeks from Greece. They do not accept each other. Eventually, once they get to know each other they will.

> They expect to find more now. They think that money grows on trees. They do not realize that we must work hard in order to succeed, to get what we have. They expect all Americans to be wealthy.

> I have become prejudiced against Greek immigrants. I do not like Greek immigrants. This bothers me terribly that I do not like Greek immigrants. I feel that the attitude of the recent immigrant is different from that of the old immigrant. I don't know why but the recent immigrant seems to offend me as a result of the way of approaching things like earning money. They are very materialistic and loud, and these two things I do not like. Those are two qualities that I dislike. A lot of them think the country here owes them something. Many of them are very critical. I dislike it when they say, "This is not so in Greece and Greece is much better than this." This bothers me. Think of the argument about the parochial school, for example, in this community, supported by recent migrants. I have given it a thought. I would not mind if they were doing it as an interim situation with the objective of improving public school, but they are doing it for nationalistic purposes, to keep Greeks together and this bothers me. We may as well build a wall around us. I feel public school is important in a free society, and we should interact with all people.

> The new migrants seem to think that America owes them something. They come over here and find everything built up for them. Everything is just ready like the churches and the communities. It is really very easy for them. They seem to me to cling very closely to the "Mother Country." The other groups have assimilated. They feel that Greeks here in Amer-

ica owe them a living or something. They seem to give the impression that they expect something for nothing.

Immigrants today are wise guys. The old migrants came with more sound purposes. Today, they expect everything laid out for them. They have to be executives. Not dishwashers. There are some sharpies, to be sure.

Completely different set of ethics and moral code between the old migrants like my parents and the present . . . A new breed . . . Loud . . . Money hungry . . . You give them a job, the next day they would be discussing additional money, fringe benefits. They want the money and facilities of the Greek communities but are unwilling to participate, help. It is almost as if it is their right.

Representative responses from third generation Greek Americans reflect, at least in part, a less antagonistic view of the recent migrant:

I feel that the newly migrated Greeks think the same as we do. The barrier is the language, other than that no difficulty in making friends. I would differentiate between Greeks that come from Greece and those that are here. Those that come now try to act more like Americans.

The recent migrants are nice people. They impress me as very meek, kind of scared. We have many in the community now.

Recent immigration? Basically, the same as early immigration. The ones I meet are progressive, not highly schooled, but successful in their own right.

New migrants are not quite as intimidated by the culture. In some ways they seem a bit too eager to Americanize their behavior. At the same time, they are not afraid to show their ethnicity. Of course, circumstances are different now. It is acceptable now to be an ethnic while in the past foreignism was embarrassing and looked down upon.

Recent migrants are also not as devoted to the Church. Perhaps they might have been disillusioned by the state of the church in Greece. They are not church centered. My parents, though born here made sure to settle near a church, within walking distance even.

I hear a lot of things from my parents and grand-parents about the newly migrated Greeks. They have some choice words to describe their attitudes and behaviors. Though I have had very little contact with recent migrants, I think it is because they expect them to think as they do or they did. They cannot stand the idea that they have modern ideas, different approach to life, different sexual attitudes, different values. They do not realize that Greece is not what they left or what they remember. They expect that the clock has stopped the moment they left Greece. I know my parents, born as they are in this country, still talk as my grandparents because that is what they were taught to believe.

I see Greekness from the point of view of heritage and from the point of view of ancient understanding. I consider Greek culture to indicate Hellenism, sophis-tication, civilization, the Hellenistic view of Greek, in a sense the view that everyone can become Greek, the philosophy of Alexander the Great. Too often, and for some people, Greek gets to denote the person who was born or whose parents were born in Greece. This limits the true meaning. To many, it is the life of their village, their dances, their peasant life, the images of Zorba the Greek. Recent migrants are the worst example. They fear Americanization, and what they see as contamination. They are possessive about their children, fearful of change, and contact with the outside world. They are paranoid about their children becoming American. They insist on the per-petuation of the peasant culture, not realizing that for their children this culture is embarrassing. It has no meaning and relevance to their lives. They are successful, yes, economically, but they give very little support to the Greek American community.

Preservation of institutions? That is a big question. We have to open up to conversions, Americanize the Church, give English lessons, create strong youth programs. Those things are not being done. We have to identify more with the American way of life and not to cater to immigrants. On the contrary, we must help them to acclimate, become members of the larger society, and not to freeze time and let them live in their own world.

Addressing specifically the issue of language and language preservation, third generation Greek Americans had this to say:

I love the Greek language. Now that I am studying history, my interest has grown. I love to eventually look further into the Byzantine and Classical times. I am studying Greek privately now, and I am enjoying it. I went to Greek afternoon school for four to five years. I did not get very much out of it. I learned something about reading and writing but not speech. My teacher was a disciplinarian, very strict. I think he was from Greece. We went for two hours, twice a week. All grades of students were together, and it was difficult to teach this way. Most of the time was spent dealing with disciplinary problems. I know it is financially problematic, and in terms of other resources difficult, but each grade should have its own teacher. They should also concentrate on the spoken language—simple stories, short stories, novels, depending on grade—making it interesting. Grammar can be taught through the spoken language. Preservation is difficult, but it is not futile, if you try with the right methods.

Greek parents send their children to Greek parochial school, but it seems to me that many do it to avoid the public schools for whatever the reasons. Then of course you have the problem of limited opportunities to study on the junior high and senior high school levels. Greeks do not seem to cooperate, to pool their resources to build up a cohesive educational system. Instead, every community strives to have its own school. Since, there is no junior and senior high school available, many Greek parents send their children to Catholic schools. I know several families who have done this.

Take the issue of the Greek language and Greek school, for example. I am all for preserving the language, but we have to redefine it. The system, as is, will not work. We have to teach Greek in a broader, relevant context with updated methods and curricula. I remember my own experience. I went to Greek school once when I was seven or eight years old. I was genuinely interested to learn, but what I found was this woman teacher who was screaming and yelling. No one was paying attention, everyone was talking and running around. There was no learning, and I decided this was not for me. I learned later on to read and write on my own, being I suppose motivated by a degree of exposure to educational materials available in my home. My parents never forced us, although Greek was used mostly as a fun experience. For a long time, I associated the Church and Greek school with some kind of craziness.

And on the subject of dating and of marriage, in and out of the group, the following responses summarize the sentiment of the second and third generation respondents, when such issues related to the recent migrant:

I find also that dating a Greek boy is different. I dated someone from Greece . . . He was always three steps ahead of me. Always trying so hard to prove he was the man, and I think being brought up here I never thought you are the man and I am the woman, and I have to listen to you. It has always been an equal give and take with me. It was obvious that he always had to have the upper hand in all situations, in what we said, in what we did, without any question. Not that I resented it, but I was not

used to it. It was very shocking. It was a very interesting experience.

Greeks "off the boat" are backward and not good
enough. I would not marry a Greek because we were
brought up in two different worlds and we would
disagree in many ways. I would not even date one.
They are the kings and want you to be submissive.

I had experience with Greek clubs in two institutions
of higher learning. The members were basically from
Greece. There were very few Greek Americans joining the clubs. I think it is because since most of the
members speak Greek, this intimidates the Greek
American students. They speak Greek all the time.
They have a different outlook. Males associate with
each other and do not consider their female counter-
parts. They are very chauvinistic. They associate and
keep company with American girls while they know
that they intend to marry a Greek girl. I have heard
a lot of stories. They keep company with Americans
while they have someone back home waiting. Occasionally, they are outsmarted.

I personally would prefer someone of Greek descent
because of a common background, especially religion.
I will not refuse or rule out the possibility to date
others. I guess my parents would like me to marry
a Greek American. If your parents give you a hard
time, trouble, it would be easier to avoid fights. I
would not rule out the possibility of dating someone
from Greece if we had common interests, and he
would bend a little to accommodate to the American
image.

Migrants had their own impressions of the native-born generations as the following statements indicate:

Greek Americans? Not being part of whatever I
call Greek history, habits, customs, language, etc.
Insecure . . . Cannot make up their mind whether
they are Greeks or Americans. I have the worst
opinion.

The interest of the native-born Greek American for
Greece is the interest of the tourist. Scenery . . .
Deeper ties very few. Most of them are not aware
of the good qualities of this nation. They have to
come in contact with people from the village to
understand.

They are Americans . . . Forget it . . . When we die,
things will be different because even the ones that
come from Greece now have changed. Where is the
old morality, the love of family and country?

The young Greek Americans have feelings and love
for Greece, but at the same time they love America
more, as their country. They try, but they have a
different orientation. Many of the children born
here try but deep down they feel and think differently.

I have lukewarm feelings about the native-born
Greek Americans. Certainly, they do not possess the
sense of obligation that characterized Greeks. They
lack respect. The young man's world is very selfish.

Yes. Antagonism exists. We have to think of it in
terms of group mentality among Greeks. I remember
so well the episode of a party where both Greeks
from Greece and Greek Americans were invited.
There was the spirit of togetherness among those
from Greece, sharing in singing and having fun.
When the group moved into the room where most
Greek Americans were present something was lost.
Singing and spirit affected. They drifted apart. We
had to go out of our way to involve them. There are
differences in orientation. Greeks always have an
opinion, are curious. Greek Americans have acquired
the Anglo-Saxon orientation, constitutional thought,
involved with privacy, safeguarding privacy. Greeks
are more extroverted, curious, giving advice.

I feel and I know others like me do, more foreign
among Greeks of America than Americans. Perhaps
it is due to the expectation that because we have
things in common, we should feel at home. We do

not have the expectation to feel at home with foreigners. In the American setting, we go and operate with logic. We expect intellectual or social cohesion. With the Greek Americans, we operate more on the emotional level. We have different expectations.

Yes, they accuse us of coming here for money. After we suffered so many invasions, and after our participation in the common cause to save the Western civilization, first against the Italians and then against the Germans, the Communists, having also been among the first ones to send troops to Korea to help what America stood for, if we had been participating in all those dangers, giving our blood for a common cause, why should we not get a reward? Since that reward has never reached Greece, we come here and expect work and money to improve our lives because our lives were endangered, and when they needed us they wanted us.

Recent migrants perceived reactions of the old migrants and the native-born rationalizing differences in perceptions as follows:

Hostility towards Greeks from Greece can be understood in terms of bitterness, frustration, and disappointment that old Greeks have experienced in the sense that they have not made it back which was their original intention. Their initial goal has not been met. Many of them wanted to save money and go back. This goal has not materialized. Frustration and bitterness is the result of failure to achieve it. To counteract frustration, they spend money to show that they made it, to prove that they made it.

Some cannot stand the idea that some newer Greeks come here to study, to go to school for the purpose of education. I remember from personal experience how I had to tell a lady off when she remarked with hostility and arrogance to the news that I had come to the United States to study. "Come just for school? And I cannot even go back to Greece after so many years?"

A Greek is unpredictable. He is not always understood. In reality, only a Greek can understand a
Greek. There are two basic traits characterizing a
Greek. First, his unlimited curiosity, desire to know,
to evaluate, and secondly, his sense of humor which
borders on sarcasm, if you will. This latter is often
misunderstood, and definitely lost by succeeding
generations that have become so called acculturated.
But for the Greek, it is a source of strength and
courage to face obstacles with laughter, turn sadness
into something more bearable, a joke.

Description of the Sample of the Second Study

Of the 102 respondents of the latest study, fifty were
females and fifty-two males. Fifty-six per cent of the sample
were in their twenties, born in the sixties, 4 per cent were
born in the seventies. Of the rest, 9 per cent were born in
the thirties, 10 per cent in the forties, and 10 per cent in the
fifties. A small percentage was born in the twenties. Of the
102 subjects, 47 per cent were born in the United States and
the rest in Greece proper with a small number born in areas
designated as "other," meaning areas previously Greek or
areas with considerable Greek population. Fifty-four per cent
of the sample included first generation Greek-Americans, 36
per cent second and 11 per cent third generation. Ninety-six
per cent reported Greek Orthodoxy as their religion. Forty-
seven per cent attended church once a month or more frequently, 14 per cent reporting once a week attendance. The
rest of the sample reported attending Church once every six
months to once or less a year. Approximately, 7 per cent
reported "never" as Church attendance.

Sixty-three per cent were single, 32 per cent married,
and the remainder widowed or divorced. Of those born
in Greece, 96 per cent attended school in Greece, 21 per
cent having completed grammar school, 14 per cent and 45
per cent junior and high school respectively. Fourteen per
cent had some college or had graduated from college, and 4
per cent had advanced degrees. Of the native-born group, 98
per cent attended school in the United States. One assumes
that the 2 per cent who were born in the United States but
did not attend school in this country represents individuals

whose families repatriated, and as a result received their education in Greece or elsewhere. Sixteen per cent of the group attained schooling at the junior and high school levels, while 82 per cent finished some college, or held advanced degrees. Only 23 per cent of the sample attended parochial school, the average attendance being two years. Most attended public school, and from those who answered this question, 60 per cent had attended Greek afternoon school from one to twelve years. Checking on intentions of sending children, to either parochial or Greek afternoon school, 45 per cent indicated parochial school and 68 per cent Greek afternoon school. The high percentage favoring parochial school is undoubtedly a reflection of the number of young migrants included in the sample. Of those responding, 93 per cent considered such training important or very important while 7 per cent considered it not very important. Reasons given included culture, tradition, roots, character strength, and other ethnically related reasons such as, religion and language.

Forty-two per cent of the respondents were students, 30 per cent professionals, 11 per cent clerical and kindred occupations. Only 50 per cent belonged to Greek organizations, 46 per cent of those organizations were characterized as Greek-American organizations, 11 per cent as Greek and 19 per cent as American Greek.

In terms of Greek language proficiency, the group's speaking ability was rated high, 64 per cent reporting speaking the language very well and 13 per cent somewhat well. Sixty per cent could read Greek very well, 15 per cent well and 6 per cent somewhat well. Writing ability was closely following the speaking ability, 52 per cent reporting they could write very well, 16 per cent well and 10 per cent they could write somewhat. Understanding the language was rated on a higher level of proficiency, 73 per cent understanding it very well, 16 per cent well and 6 per cent somewhat. Language proficiency reflected sample representation predominantly comprised of migrant Greeks and second generation Greek Americans.

With regard to ethnic identification, 33 per cent of the group identified themselves as Greek, 34 per cent as Greek Americans and 24 per cent as American Greeks, 5 per cent as "other," and 2 per cent as Cypriots. Sixty-one per cent assessed their ethnic identification as very strong, 26 per cent as strong, 10 per cent as somewhat strong, and only 1 per

cent as "not at all." In answer to the question of how others
viewed them, 31 per cent thought that they were views as
Greek, 32 per cent as Greek Americans, 22 per cent as American Greek, and 6 per cent as American, 3 per cent as "other,"
and 4 per cent as Cypriots. It is of interest to note that some
of the Cypriots wished to distinguish themselves as Cypriots
rather than Greek.

An attempt was made to ascertain political views, the
group leaning heavily on political views of the Center, 29 per
cent left of Center and 49 per cent Center. Twenty-two per
cent indicated conservatism and a right of Center identification. The majority of the respondents would not vote for a
Greek running for office (70%) regardless of political affiliation.

The sample of the study adhered to endogamy, 64 per cent
reporting dating Greek, Greek American, American Greeks,
and only 32 per cent Americans or others (other ethnic
groups). If unmarried, 74 per cent would prefer a Greek,
Greek American or American Greek as a spouse. Preference
for non-Greeks leaned more toward other ethnics. The major
reasons given included "sharing same background," "better
communication," "children's heritage," other such commonality
reasons and "to please parents." The spouses of those married
were identified as Greek, Greek American, American Greek
(35 per cent, 13 per cent, and 20 per cent, respectively). Ten
per cent were identified as Cypriots and 13 per cent as "other."
The high intra-group dating and marriage reflects sampling
limitations as the level is considerably higher than statistics
for the group indicate. Table II describes some of the descriptive variables comparing the native-born and foreign-born
respondents.

TABLE 2

DEMOGRAPHIC AND DESCRIPTIVE VARIABLES FOR THE SECOND STUDY

Variables		Sample N	Sample %	Native-Born N	Native-Born %	Foreign-Born N	Foreign-Born %	X²	df	Sample Size	Significance
Sex	Male	52	51.0	23	47.9	29	53.7	0.15	1	102	N.S.
	Female	50	49.0	25	52.1	25	46.3				
Generational Status	First	54	53.5	0	0.0	54	100.0	101.00	1	101	p<.001
	Second	36	35.6	36	76.6	0	0.0				
	Third	11	10.9	11	23.4	0	0.0				
Marital	Never Married	63	63.0	28	58.3	35	67.5	1.08	3	100	N.S.
	Married	32	32.0	17	35.4	15	28.8				
	Divorced	2	2.0	1	21.0	1	1.9				
	Widowed	3	3.0	2	4.2	1	1.9				
	Separated	0	0.0	0	0.0	0	0.0				
Occupation	Professional	31	30.4	21	43.8	10	18.5	16.70	9	102	p<.05
	M.O.P. (Managers officials, proprietors)	2	2.0	1	2.1	1	1.9				
	Clerical and Kindred workers, sales workers	11	10.8	7	14.6	4	7.4				
	Small shopkeepers	2	2.0	0	0.0	2	3.7				
	Craftsmen, formen, and kindred workers	2	2.0	0	0.0	2	3.7				
	Unskilled, operative service workers	4	3.9	0	0.0	4	7.4				
	Students	43	42.2	15	31.3	28	51.0				
	Housewives	2	2.0	1	2.1	1	1.9				
	None (unemployed)	2	2.0	1	2.1	1	1.9				
	No Response	3	2.9	2	4.2	1	1.9				

TABLE 2 (continued)

Variables		Sample N	Sample %	Native-Born N	Native-Born %	Foreign-Born N	Foreign-Born %	X^2	df	Sample Size	Significance
Total Number of Organizations (Membership)	1	25	35.7	7	21.2	18	48.6	9.84	5	70	N.S.
	2	29	41.4	15	45.5	14	37.8				
	3	8	11.4	5	15.2	3	8.1				
	4	6	8.6	5	15.2	1	2.7				
	5	1	1.4	1	3.0	0	0.0				
	6	1	1.4	0	0.0	1	2.7				
Greek Organizations (Membership)	yes	47	50.0	26	27.7	21	23.3	2.74	1	94	N.S.
	no	47	50.0	17	18.1	30	31.9				
Voting for Greek American	yes	28	30.1	6	14.0	22	44.0	8.54	1	93	p<.004
	no	65	69.9	37	86.0	28	56.0				
Parochial School Attendance	yes	20	23.3	13	30.2	7	16.3	1.63	1	86	N.S.
	no	66	76.7	30	69.8	36	83.7				
Parochial School Attendance for Children	yes	40	44.9	13	27.1	27	65.9	11.91	1	89	p<.001
	no	49	55.1	35	72.9	14	34.1				
Importance of Greek School	Very important	36	48.6	12	34.3	24	61.5	7.56	3	74	p<.05
	Important	33	44.6	19	54.4	14	35.9				
	Not very important	3	4.1	3	8.6	0	0.0				
	Not at all important	2	2.7	1	2.9	1	2.6				
Greek Identity	Greek	32	33.0	2	4.4	30	57.7	46.49	5	97	p<.001
	Greek American	33	34.0	19	42.2	14	26.9				
	American Greek	23	23.7	21	46.7	2	3.8				
	American	2	2.1	2	4.4	0	0.0				
	Other	5	5.2	1	2.2	4	7.7				
	Cypriot	2	2.1	0	0.0	2	3.8				

TABLE 2 (continued)

Variables	Sample N	Sample %	Native-Born N	Native-Born %	Foreign-Born N	Foreign-Born %	X²	df	Sample Size	Significance
Identity View by Others							44.68	6	99	p < .001
Greek	31	31.3	4	8.9	27	50.0				
Greek American	32	32.3	12	26.7	20	37.0				
American Greek	22	22.2	20	44.4	2	3.7				
American	6	6.1	6	13.3	0	0.0				
Other	3	3.0	2	4.4	1	1.9				
Cypriot	4	4.0	0	0.0	4	7.4				
No response	1	1.0	1	2.2	0	0.0				
Dating							21.91	5	89	p < .001
Greek	26	29.2	3	7.3	23	47.9				
Greek American	24	27.0	16	39.0	8	16.7				
American Greek	7	7.9	5	12.2	2	4.2				
American	13	14.6	9	22.0	4	8.3				
Other	15	16.9	7	17.1	8	16.7				
Cypriot	4	4.5	1	2.4	3	6.3				
Future Spouse							29.80	5	70	p < .001
Greek	22	31.4	2	6.5	20	51.3				
Greek American	21	30.0	14	45.2	7	17.9				
American Greek	9	12.9	8	25.8	1	2.6				
American	3	4.3	3	9.7	0	0.0				
Other	11	15.7	4	12.9	7	17.9				
Cypriot	4	5.7	0	0.0	4	10.3				

Findings of the Second Study (N = 102)

 Responses in the second study support the following portraits of Greeks, Greek Americans, American Greeks and Americans as perceived by the groups of native-born and foreign-born Greek Americans. They are to be sure similarities in their portraits, but also differences that set them somewhat apart as they perceive their world through their subjective culture. The native-born group consisted of 23 second generation and 10 third generation respondents who answered this section of the questionnaire. They were asked what characteristics they liked best and least for Greeks, Greek Americans, American Greeks, and Americans. This native-born group listed warmth, friendliness, gregariousness, loyalty to heritage, family and child centeredness, hospitality, spontaneity, and zest for life when rating Greeks. They admired their pursuit for education, political astuteness, pride, alertness, patriotism, humor, philosophical leanings, work ethic, ambition, optimism, compassion, romanticism, sexiness, honesty, and straight forwardness. Family orientation, traditionalism, culture and heritage with specific emphasis on language preservation were the predominating responses in the best liked category.

 Greeks were disliked on the other hand by the native-born for their dishonesty, deceitfulness, suspiciousness of their leaders and institutions, lack of respect for time and commitments, narrow-mindedness, prejudice with regard to other groups, and ethnic exclusiveness. Least liked attributes include sexism, nationalism, with regard to Greece, and ethnocentrism. They are perceived as money hungry, authoritarian, opinionated, ethnically chauvinistic, selfish, stiflingly dependent on family, irresponsible, inflexible, rude, crude, loud, superstitious, aggressive, indirect in their communication, egocentric, clannish, stubborn, and insular. They are disliked for their pessimism, disorganization, xenophilia, deviousness, parochialism, paranoia, manipulation, arrogance, past orientation, and unwillingness to accept the customs of their adopted country. Some see them as suspicious, bigots, and jealous of each other. Narrowmindedness and ethnocentrism predominate as least liked characteristics.

 Interestingly, perceptions held for Greek Americans and American Greeks depended on their placement by the perceiving groups on the acculturation/assimilation continuum. Greek Americans to a great extent were perceived as possessing characteristics similar to those of the Greeks with favorable acknowledgement of their bicultural accommodation, their ability to successfully balance the two worlds. With regard to their connection to ethnic roots, religious observance and community organizational involvement were repeatedly mentioned as best liked characteristics. In addition, Greek Americans are admired for their resourcefulness, pragmatism, achievement, and characteristics increasingly reflecting the American value of upward mobility. American Greeks perceived closer to the American stereotype are best liked for their sense of responsibility, fair mindedness, liberalism, open-mindedness, utilitarianism, openness to people while maintaining distance, task orientation, flexibility and dependability. They are admired for their resolution of ethnic identity issues, and for their assimilation into the mainstream of American society while respecting elements of their culture, admittedly with a reduced sense of history. American Greeks are perceived by the native-born groups as holding a more progressive view of relationships, an American brand of Hellenism, "a sense of tradition without going overboard," and a sentimental attachment to their culture. They are goal oriented, have direction, cool temperment, and directness. They are charitable and tolerable of differences.

Americans are perceived as having many of the favorable characteristics attributed to American Greeks with much emphasis on freedom, independence, success orientation, flexibility, gentleness, generosity, open-mindedness, humility, an easy going and positive attitude and a work ethic.

With regard to least liked attributes the native-borns rated Greek American least liked characteristics similarly to those attributed to Greeks, although such attributes are expressed in a toned down intensity. Ethnic exclusiveness and clannishness are characteristics least liked for Greeks and are also least liked for Greek Americans (e.g., "Greek Americans can be too interested in Greek tradition, therefore, they are sometimes ethnically exclusive"). Greek Americans are liked least by the native-born subgroupings for their religious affiliation as a status symbol, the syrtaki/souvlaki syndrome and all its implications. They are faulted for their achievement motivation at the expense of children, their bourgeois obsession with the work ethic, diplomas, and their concern of how things look to the community. They are perceived as marginal, uncommitted, ambivalent and indecisive especially with regard to ethnic identity. They are least liked for their unwillingness to expand their horizons beyond the Greek American community. Greek Americans are seen as uncomfortable with themselves and looking down on Greeks and everything Greek.

American Greeks are placed closer to the American side on the continuum of Greekness and Americanism. They are perceived as invisible, mainstream, and confused about heritage and family values. They are obsessed with money and with being "au courant." They are present and/or future oriented, secretive, self-centered, and utilitarian in orientation. They are lacking in warmth and are faulted for intermarriage, lacking pride in their heritage, family detachment, and mostly for ethnic language indifference and snobbishness toward the recent migrant. American Greeks are like least for wishing to be Americans and identifying more with Americans. They are perceived as being apolitical, cold, naive, parsimonious, lacking in global perspective, individualistic, condescending, reserved and uninterested in other cultures.

Thirty-one foreign-born respondents shared their perceptions of best and least liked characteristics attributed to Greeks, Greek Americans, American Greeks, and Americans. Interestingly, they were more willing to deal with the best liked than the least liked characteristics. In addition, they seem more willing to express themselves and to describe Greeks and Greek Americans while ignoring for the most part the subgroupings of American Greeks and Americans as if they were indeed the "others" (i.e., the outgroup). In general, responses reflected patterns of exclusion and inclusion with regard to the native-born groups. There was more of a tendency to ascribe similar characteristics to Greeks and Greek Americans at times perceiving themselves as Greek Americans or American Greeks as Greeks. American Greeks were more often than not excluded of ethnic identification and perceived as Americans in both the best and least liked characteristics.

The foreign-born group rated Greeks and Greek Americans as best liked for their philotimo, with a stronger identification of this characteristic attributed to Greeks. The two groups were also acknowledged positively for their knowledge of the Greek language, such knowledge expressed in probability terms in the case of Greek Americans. Both groups were admired for their group cohesiveness, sense of belongingness, their identification with Greek ethnicity, loyalty to Greek ideals, intensity, family orientation, and patriotism. Greek Americans and American Greeks were seen progressively as more liberal, more flexible, more in touch with the American system, and more neutral with regard to ethnic issues. Religion was more closely related to Greek Americans and to a certain extent to American Greeks. As mentioned, earlier American Greeks were seen more and more as shifting toward the direction of Americanism, although some respondents understood the inherent difficulty in defining such a diverse and amorphous group.

On the best liked category of attributes, American Greeks and Americans shared attributes of open-mindednes, honesty, independence, liberalism, dependability, efficiency, sincerity, and sensitivity. They are seen as conscientious, understanding, prompt and achieving. To some of the foreign-born respondents, American Greeks were seen as Americanized, but "at least they do not call themselves Americans." American-Greeks share gregariousness with Americans, have less "hang-ups," are gentle and easy going.

On the negative side, the foreign-born groups faulted Greeks for their xenophilia, suspiciousness, stubborness, narrow-mindedness, inflexibility, conservatism, irresponsibility (especially in business dealings), snobbishness, a tendency to ridicule, and a "know-it-all" attitude. They were perceived as boisterous, authoritarian, not serious enough, intent on speaking the Greek language, egotistical, cunning, abrupt, and lazy. They were seen as megalomaniacs and in many ways rated similarly by the native-born group. Greek Americans were perceived as possessing similar negative characteristics in addition to being seen as more parochial, more envious of neighbors, more materialistic and prone to gossip. Prominent were the perception of marginality, the poor knowledge of the Greek language, the snobbishness toward the recent migrant, the contempt held for those who speak English with an accent, the inability to organize for a common goal, the jealousy of the success of others, and especially those who have moved to the U.S. recently. American Greeks are perceived as lacking pride in their heritage. They were like Americans independent, impatient, inconsiderate, impolite, selfish, permissive, passive, naive, parsimonious, cold, distant, future oriented, task oriented at the exclusion of process, apolitical and lacking in global perspective. In summary, the perceptions of the native-born and foreign-born subgroupings showed no clear dichotomies and contrasting world views.

A point of interest could be said to be the extensiveness of characteristics attributed to each group, perhaps understood in terms of the complexity of ethnicity definition and identity conceptualization. Stereotypes are presented by multiple, ambivalent, and imperfectly articulated criteria of identification. In addition, while respondents spoke freely about their perceptions of the characteristics of the subgroupings in interviews, they had some difficulty listing specific traits, best liked or least liked for each group. Their responses seemed to project emotional rather than cognitive understanding. Antipathies were based upon inflexible generalizations, each subgrouping assuming that the other's beliefs and values are incongruent with its own when in fact they were not so different. It seems that no one group can claim to possess the truth for Greekness or Americanism, but perception of these groups is relative to the immigration status and the experiences of the perceiver.

The second part of this study examined subjects' ratings of 23 descriptive characteristics on a 1 to 10 bipolar scale for Greek, Greek American, American Greek, and American groups. The data were analyzed using an analysis of variance for group differences. The findings are presented in Table 3. Out of the 23 variables tested six proved to be statistically significant. They included present oriented/past oriented, flexible/inflexible, open-minded/narrow-minded, gentle/crude, dance interested/uninterested in dance, and patriotic/unpatriotic.

With regard to present oriented/past oriented, both native-born and foreign-born research participants rated past oriented significantly higher for Greeks. The foreign-born gave a higher rating for all groups favoring past oriented. The native-born saw this orientation shifting progressively to a present oriented outlook as one moved along the ethnic identification continuum from Greek to American. The flexible/inflexible variable reflected a distribution similar to time orientation. The native-born rated inflexibility progressively changing to flexibility as one views the subgroupings in Amer-

TABLE 3

ANALYSIS OF VARIANCE OF PERSONAL CHARACTERISTICS
OF GREEKS, GREEK AMERICANS, AMERICAN GREEKS, AND AMERICANS

Characteristics	Native/ Foreign Born	Greek	Greek American	American Greek	American	F	df
Hard working/ Lazy	N	3.78	3.15	3.50	3.86	1.52	3,85
	F	4.79	5.25	5.46	6.23		
Active/ Inactive	N	4.22	3.93	3.47	3.81	2.16	3,85
	F	5.02	5.30	5.18	6.13		
Independent/ Dependent	N	4.11	4.29	3.54	3.31	1.72	3,85
	F	5.39	5.09	5.67	5.25		
Present Oriented/ Past Oriented	N	5.79	4.77	3.56	3.00	3.12*	3,85
	F	6.32	5.25	5.27	5.30		
Flexible/ Inflexible	N	6.25	5.47	4.04	3.38	6.04**	3,85
	F	5.53	5.76	5.23	5.58		
Honest/ Deceitful	N	4.90	4.46	3.75	3.85	0.95	3,81
	F	5.61	5.35	5.30	5.47		
Open Minded/ Narrow Minded	N	6.31	5.53	3.73	3.34	6.62**	3,81
	F	5.76	5.73	5.92	5.47		
Gentle/ Crude	N	5.71	5.16	5.78	4.97	2.60*	3,81
	F	5.46	5.06	4.85	4.63		
Quiet/ Boisterous	N	6.21	5.24	4.43	4.04	1.05	3,81
	F	6.66	5.90	5.69	5.64		
Trustful/ Mistrustful	N	5.48	5.05	4.17	4.12	1.46	3,80
	F	5.79	5.51	5.67	5.11		
Generous/ Cheap	N	4.33	4.61	4.10	4.69	1.77	3,80
	F	5.00	5.37	6.02	6.16		
Ambitious/ Not Ambitious	N	3.64	3.43	3.82	3.89	0.10	3,80
	F	4.79	4.90	5.23	5.18		

TABLE 3 (continued)
ANALYSIS OF VARIANCE OF PERSONAL CHARACTERISTICS
OF GREEKS, GREEK AMERICANS, AMERICAN GREEKS, AND AMERICANS

Characteristics	Native/ Foreign Born	Greek	Greek American	American Greek	American	F	df
Dance Interest/ Uninterested	N	3.25	3.41	4.41	5.43	2.12*	3,80
	F	4.58	4.97	5.18	5.37		
Nationalistic/ Universalist	N	3.07	3.97	4.53	4.84	0.90	3,80
	F	3.93	5.48	5.48	5.16		
Patriotic/ Unpatriotic	N	3.34	2.42	2.47	2.47	2.71*	3,81
	F	2.89	2.52	2.33	2.83		
Family Centered/ Family Independent	N	3.25	3.37	4.05	5.17	1.26	3,81
	F	4.00	4.81	5.83	5.64		
Liberal/ Conservative	N	5.00	5.13	5.90	5.41	2.08	3,81
	F	5.30	5.84	5.40	5.10		
Authoritarian/ Permissive	N	3.15	4.10	5.22	5.75	1.32	3,81
	F	4.30	5.51	5.74	5.93		
Materialistic/ Not Materialistic	N	4.67	4.25	4.55	4.15	0.24	3,81
	F	5.30	5.25	5.06	4.95		
Aggressive/ Passive	N	4.21	4.26	4.63	4.39	0.97	3,79
	F	4.40	5.47	4.97	5.15		
Proud/ Humble	N	3.39	3.31	3.82	4.14	0.62	3,79
	F	4.07	4.82	5.30	5.45		
Achieving/ Non-Achieving	N	3.70	2.95	3.31	3.41	0.67	3,79
	F	4.75	4.75	5.07	5.02		
Gregarious/ Self-Contained	N	4.09	4.87	4.75	5.19	0.25	3,81
	F	5.52	6.02	5.83	5.30		

Note: Characteristics were rated on a bipolar 10-point scale.
*$p < .05$
**$p < .001$

icanization terms, Greek Americans seen as more flexible than Greeks, American Greeks more flexible than Greek Americans, and Americans as the most flexible of all.

The foreign-born rated subgroupings almost the same, apparently perceiving themselves as flexible as everybody else. Native-born Greek Americans perceive Greeks as narrow-minded shifting this perception progressively in favor of Greek Americans, American Greeks and most of all Americans who are perceived considerably more open-minded. The foreign-born groups show practically no difference in their perceptions rating everyone more toward the center and holding themselves in line with everybody else.

Gentleness is more characteristic of Americans according to both native and foreign-born groupings. The foreign-born group attributed a degree of gentleness to American Greeks in line with the qualitative data indicating that for the foreign-born American Greeks approximate Americans in many of the best and least liked characteristic.

Love of dance has been closely identified with Greekness and the variable emerged as significant in this analysis of data as well. Greeks and Greek Americans are closely rated as dance loving by the native-born who in turn see this attribute as progressively diminishing as one moves toward the Americanism continuum. The foreign-born groups viewed Greeks and Greek Americans more dance loving than American Greeks and Americans, but assessed American Greeks and Americans as more similar than the native-born group's rating.

With regard to patriotism, the native-born made a clear distinction between Greeks and the other three subgroupings having perceived the former as somewhat less patriotic. Patriotism for Greek Americans, American Greeks and Americans was rated similarly. The foreign-born rated Greeks and Americans as slightly less patriotic than Greek Americans and American Greeks.

Surprisingly, other variables which predominated in the data analysis of the first qualitative study presented in this paper, did not prove to be of statistical significance. Yet, there is at times, a suggested direction supportive of the qualitative data.

In general, the statistical analysis indicated that it was the native-born group that made distinctions between the four groups they were asked to rate. The foreign-born sample rated the four groups as more similar than different. As with the first study, the perception of "Greekness" or "Americanism" was determined by the assimilation and immigration status of the perceiver.

DISCUSSION

Generalizing from the interview material, looked upon generationally, the generational groups of the investigation present two types of split, that of the foreign-born and the native-born. Within this split, there appears to be another split that of the old migrant and the more recent migrant. Though there appears to be reciprocity in the feeling of antagonism, the reaction of old migrants and the second generation toward the recent migrant, as a matter of degree, is harsher. Statements of the respondents unmistakably speak of stereotypic views the subgroupings of the ethnic community hold of each other, each drawing ethnic identification from a different frame of reference. The fact becomes progressively apparent that when one speaks of the Greek American subcommunity in the United States, one would have to acknowledge a new brand of Hellenism. Antagonism is in evidence, directed mainly toward the recent migrant by both the old migrants and the native-born generation respondents. The findings are suggestive of several explanations. Firstly, the first generation cannot see themselves as they were then, since inevitably, and however slowly, the acculturative process has made inroads. Secondly, the old migrants may be rejecting a picture that was unpleasant and rejected by others. In an attempt to safeguard their values, they have clung to a past which no longer exists even in their native Greece, a past that has been idealized and held unaltered in a myth-reality interplay while values have changed in Greece after at least two major world wars, foreign occupation, internal upheavals, increased outside contact, education, industrialization, urbanization and social change. In a paper entitled "Historical Trends in Greek Migration to the United States," Vlachos addresses the issue of "strain of 'oldtimers,' traditional in outlook and hardworking and the 'newcomers,' whom in the opinion of some Greek Americans found the table 'all set.'" (Vlachos, 1976). Vlachos points to the status differential of the two subgroupings, the recent migrants having come to the United States "relatively young, in a more equalized sex ratio, of higher education, and of predominantly urban origin" (p. 15). And many of the new arrivals have arrived in this country as married couples with small children and many of the women have themselves entered the labor market (Moskos, 1980). As for relations between the American-born Greeks and the new migrants, Moskos considers them more problematic in the sense that "excepting relatives most of the second and third generations come into contact with new Greeks only at church services and Greek American social affairs. The social distance between the American-born and the new Greeks finds expression in diverse ways. There is the bemoaning of the apparent unwillingness of the new migrant arrivals to contribute either time or money to Greek Orthodox parishes or Greek American associations." (p. 60). As for the new Greek immigrant, he is dismayed by the lack of Hellenic consciousness. Moskos contends that the negative stereotype many American-born Greeks hold of the recent migrants can be understood as a form of filial respect for their parents and grandparents. In their eyes, the new arrivals must meet the idealized standard they hold for the earlier generation of immigrants to whom they have ascribed attributes of moral rectitude, self-sacrifice, feelings for family, and commitment to Greek American institutions.

Specifically focusing on the second generation, one may speculate that they may conceivably be rejecting the stigma of foreignism in an attempt to escape past painful experiences. To them, new migrants do not represent their Hellenism because it is a different brand of Hellenism, and they greet it with contempt. As the offspring of the old migrant generation, they shared directly or indirectly the experiences of their parents, whether conflict concerned a family situation or a community matter. They seem to bear the scars and feel antagonistic to whatever they perceive as deviation of the values with which they were socialized.

The recent arrivals are more socially conscious, better educated. Many of them have had members of their families already established here and in a position to help them to make an easier adjustment. The Greek American communities are organized and functioning for the recent migrant to avail himself of services. Some of the newcomers have had the wrong impressions about life and work in this country, have been adverse to hard work, a cause of infuriation to early immigrants who remember their own sufferings and sacrifices.

Few might have come with the idea of sharing the wealth of the rich relatives. For their part, rich relatives might have brought them over with ulterior motives of exploitation. Accusations of aggressiveness have been shared in the interviews against the newcomer and displeasure at his interference in the affairs of the Greek community. This is especially true with regard to Greek language instruction and the functioning of both Greek parochial and afternoon schools. Newcomers allegedly know best, being genuinely Greek as opposed to Americanized Greeks. New immigrants express resentment at what they perceive as lack of recognition and appreciation of their intentions. In their disappointment, they tend to emphasize the lack of refinement of older migrants and the boorish characteristics of possession of money without the proper knowledge for its use (Saloutos, 1957). It should be mentioned at this point that "if the new immigrants do not participate in the Greek American community to the purported degree of the older immigrants this is largely due to the fact that it is a community which they did not shape and whose control has increasingly entered the hands of the American-born generations" (Moskos, 1980, p. 61).

The new migrants realize that there is a strangeness, and subtly or not so subtly point to the "Americans." The third generation, more secure in its identification shows less animosity. To them, new migrants are newcomers, people like them, depending on the age, separated by the language barrier but often with the same ideals and aspirations.

It would seem that the bitterness, especially on the part of the old migrants and the second generation, touches deeper into psychological aspects of self-image and is a conflict of value orientations, a strain of coping with divergent or conflicting value systems and role expectations, contending forces of ethnic mobilization and assimilation. Antagonistic pronouncements with regard to relations between generations speak to the varying degrees to which value orientations are abandoned in favor of the adoption of the values of the dominant culture, and the partial success of intragroup structural changes in resolving the discordance between traditional and American values (Papajohn and Spiegel, 1975). Hellenism is defined differently with brands of Hellenism not always compatible. While the native-born generations and the acculturated old migrants vacillate between a past that no longer exists and a present to which they may not have quite adjusted, the new migrants are the carriers of new values, old values that have been reshaped by the passage of time, and values that through the course of historical events might have changed beyond recognition. Looking at ethnicity from the perspective of the Greek American subcommunity, one reaches an "ethnogenetic" understanding of Greek American identity, an on-going process where various generations are differently socialized into an ethnic identity. The emerging Hellenism is not the Hellenism of the homeland, but a conscious selection in an endless number of gradations in the choice of identity. According to Vlachos (1976), the Greek American subcommunity is gradually and progressively finding modified forms of perpetuating the ethnic past within the context of a pluralistic American society.

The subcultural variability reflected in the qualitative data is supported to a degree by the quantitative analysis of variance of psychosocial variables. It appears that the subgroupings give different weights to different types of information from the environment, have somewhat different priorities, and perceive their social milieu differently. Their subjective culture, the norms, roles, values, beliefs, attitudes, ideals, ways of categorizing experiences, in short, their relationship to the man-made environment, is interpreted differently or similarly according to the individual's internalizations which may correspond but are not necessarily identical to those representing all subgroupings of the Greek American community. Similarities and variances are shaped by historical and ecological factors. Triandis (1980) observes that, "Once values have changed in a certain direction they increase the probability of behaviors that will in themselves change culture." (p. 200). Through the acculturation process individuals and subgroupings within the ethnic community develop new sets of reference points which enable them to define who they are, what they are, and where they belong. Such sets differ for individuals and subgroupings. Some have been affected more than others by the course of acculturation, assimilation and Americanization. In fact, for some the influence is such that they are fewer differences between them and other Americans as the responses in the present study clearly indicate. Thus, the sentiments of social and culture orientations of Greek Americans is shifting as one moves along the generational continuum from the ethnic subculture to the dominant American society. As the dominant society becomes a positive reference group, its norms, beliefs, values modify and guide the behavior of Greek Americans. Since the rates of acculturation/assimilation/Americanization differ for individuals and subgroupings, there are distinct new definitions of ethnicity, new modes of behavior, new approaches to problems, and new roles and attitudes, which differ, either in reality or the perception of reality, from the ethnic tradition.

In view of the variability and inevitability of the acculturation/assimilation/Americanization processes is it possible to restore a unified sense of identity? Even if one assumes this is ever possible, it would require an understanding of each subgrouping's behavior, not as disturbed behavior or deviance, but as difference in perceptions and as reactions stemming from different frames of reference with regard to defining Americanism and Greekness. Intergroup behavior involves all systems of human social action, the personality system, the social environment, and the culture.

It is often difficult to understand the meaning of behavior without the necessary knowledge and appreciation of the value orientations of the individuals and subgroupings. The same behavior may have different meaning depending on one's subjective culture, one's perception of the social environment, and one's unique definition of ethnic identity. It is the intention of undertakings such as the present study to underscore the reasons for the variability of ethnic identification definition, to help subgroupings recognize the extensiveness and intensity of their ethnic identification, and to better appreciate the reasons for their value orientation as to be able to resolve conflicts that evolve out of different experiences, perceptions, and subjective culture specificities. Cross-fertilization could enhance prospects of organizational effectiveness, educational opportunities, and appreciation of a contextually determined Hellenism. While intergroup conflict is recognized we must not be left with the impression that there is no collaboration among the subgroupings, common and sharing in "a strong motivation to succeed in American society while retaining the abiding pride in . . . Hellenic heritage" (Moskos, 1980, p. 61).

REFERENCES

Costantakos, C. M. (1980). Ethnic language as a variable in subcultural continuity. In H. J. Psomiades & A. Scourby (Eds.), *The Greek American Community in transition* (pp. 137-170). New York: Pella.

Fitzpatrick, J. P. (1971). *Puerto Rican Americans: The meaning of migration to the mainland*. Englewood Cliffs, NJ: Prentice-Hall.

Fong, S. (1973). Assimilation of changing social roles of Chinese Americans. *Journal of Social Issues, 29,* 115-125.

Glaser, B., & Strauss, A. (1967). *The discovery of grounded theory: Strategies for qualitative research*. Chicago: Aldine.

Kitano, H. L. (1969). *Japanese Americans: The evolution of a subculture* (2nd ed.). Englewood Cliffs, NJ: Prentice-Hall.

Lopato, H. (1976). *Polish Americans: Status competition in an ethnic community*. Englewood Cliffs, NJ: Prentice-Hall.

Moskos, C. C. (1980). *Greek Americans: Struggle and success*. Englewood, Cliffs, NJ: Prentice-Hall.

Papajohn, J., & Spiegel, J. (1975). *Transactions in families*. San Francisco, CA: Jossey-Bass.

Saloutos, T. (1967). The Greeks in America. In C. L. Lord (Ed.), *A student's guide to localized history*. New York: Teachers College.

Scourby, A. (1980). Three generations of Greek Americans: A study in ethnicity. *International Migration Review, 14,* 43-52.

Triandis, H. C. (1972). *The analysis of subjective culture*. New York: Wiley.

Triandis, H. C. (1976). Social psychology and cultural analysis. In L. H. Stricklan, E. F. Aboud, & K. L. Gergen (Eds.), *Social psychology in transition*. New York: Plenum.

Triandis, H. C. (1980). Values, attitudes, and interpersonal behavior. In *Nebraska symposium on motivation, 1979 Vol. 27* (pp. 195-259). Lincoln City, Nebraska: University of Nebraska.

Weiss, M. S. (1970). Selective acculturation and the dating process: The patterning of Chinese Caucasian interracial dating. *Journal of Marriage and the Family, 32,* 273-280.

Vassiliou, G., & Vassiliou, V. (1973). Subjective culture and psychotherapy. *American Journal of Psychotherapy, 27,* 42-51.

Vlachos, E. (1976, October). Historical trends in Greek migration to the United States. Paper presented at the National Bicentennial Symposium on the Greek Experience in America, Chicago.

CHAPTER 4

GREEK BILINGUAL EDUCATION: POLICIES AND POSSIBILITIES

JOHN SPIRIDAKIS

Bilingual education is not a unitary treatment. Insofar as public school bilingual programs, the term "bilingual education" refers to a wide array of instructional models for teaching students who share a mutual mother tongue and whose proficiency in English is limited. Ethnolinguistic minority children are referred to as limited English proficient (LEP) as compared to their English proficient (EP) peers who are majority language speakers (Ramirez, 1985). The various models of bilingual programs also include those geared for language majority students learning a minority language as a subject, or in an "immersion" program wherein the minority or second language is used as the medium of instruction for teaching academic subjects to majority language speakers (EPs) (Ovando and Collier, 1985).

Two distinct Greek-English bilingual education program types currently exist, one in the realm of public education and the other in the realm of parochial or private school education. This article discusses (1) the status of public and parochial Greek-English bilingual education programs; (2) the societal ethnic language policies which have helped shape each type of program; (3) key pedagogical and political issues that affect the condition of these programs and, (4) the future possibilities of developing Greek-English bilingualism in the United States as a result of these programs.

Comparisons and contrasts between the public and private Greek-English bilingual education program goals and structures are elaborated for the purpose of illuminating the salient differences between the two systems of education and each system's basic characteristics and contribution to the development of the Greek American students' bilingual and cognitive/academic development. The controversy surrounding public school bilingual programs is also analyzed. The programs in New York City where Greek bilingual education in both public and parochial educational institutions is most prevalent, are focused upon.

Greek Bilingual Education Under Ethnic Community Auspices

In the United States, according to the National Center for Education Statistics (NCES) survey, Greek is considered one of the active languages. Approximately seventy percent of Greek American households use the Greek language in varying degrees, while approximately thirty percent of such households are monolingual English speakers. The NCES survey estimates 500,000 to 750,000 households in the U.S. where the Greek language is used (Waggoner, 1980; Grosjean, 1985).

In response to the desire to maintain their mother or ethnic tongue and culture, Greek Americans in the United States developed school programs so that their children could learn the Greek language and heritage. These primarily religious-sponsored Greek schools, which were initially established in Chicago at the turn of the century, were geared to providing Greek language, cultural, historical and religious education (Saloutos, 1964).

Today, most of these schools are located in New York City and are sponsored by the community Greek Orthodox Churches. As Costantakos (1982) notes, "The Greek language holds symbolic meaning in ethnic identification . . . Such a linguistic form provides the group with solidarity and cohesiveness . . . attitudes toward ethnic language remain positive despite considerable erosion, generally, in language maintenance." (p. 157). The day schools or afternoon programs are independently administered, having their own boards of education and personnel for the most part. The Greek Orthodox Archdiocese lends support to the development of these Greek community schools and programs through the providing of textbooks, the recruitment of teachers, and curriculum and staff development (Spiridakis, 1987).

In the parochial day school programs, the Greek language curriculum forms approximately fifteen percent of the daily bilingual curriculum as subject matter. Greek is not used as a medium of instruction. Afternoon Greek school programs offer a range of two to ten periods of Greek language and history to children after their regular school day in the public school (Spiridakis, 1978).

The purposes of the Greek day or afternoon schools are to foster the Greek language and culture among second, third and even fourth generation Greek Americans. These schools are a testament to the Greek ethnic vitality of any given community in which they are found. While research has criticized, appropriately, weaknesses in the administration, personnel, curriculum, and instructional strategies found in these "community-run" parochial schools, they remain a major potential force for the preservation of the Greek language in New York and the rest of the United States (Spiridakis, 1978; Fishman, 1980). In addition, these schools reflect an attempt to preserve cherished cultural values, customs and ideals of the Greek community, especially the value of education itself. While bilingualism and biculturalism are the ostensible goals of these schools, the student outcome insofar as bilingualism or the development of Greek language proficiency is concerned, vary for a variety of reasons not the least of which is the overall pressure toward Americanization which is so strongly rooted in American society and which the curricula of these schools transmit to the students in direct and indirect ways. In addition, the development of full bilingualism and ethnic language development cannot realistically be expected to occur without strong ethnic language support and reinforcement from the community (Massialas, 1984; Spiridakis, 1978).

Greek Bilingual Education in the Public Schools

While the Greek parochial schools were created and are still geared primarily toward maintaining the ethnic language and culture of the community, the use of the Greek language which arose in the public schools during the mid-seventies represented different purposes and addressed a different population of Greek American students.

From the Civil Rights movement of the sixties evolved important legislation which was to affect Greek and other language minority students. The Civil Rights Act of 1965 and the Elementary and Secondary Education Act of 1965 addressed the needs of these language minority students. New influxes of immigrants, especially Hispanics, caused school districts to seek ways to educate these non-English proficient populations. Experimental programs initially emerged for Hispanic children using bilingual instruction in regions with large numbers of LEP children (Schneider, 1976).

In 1968 the Bilingual Education Act was approved by Congress (Title VII of the 1965 Elementary and Secondary Education Act.) By the Fall of 1968, there were 56 bilingual projects in 13 states receiving federal funds. Funds increased each year to reach a high of 166.9 million for the nation's projects in 1980 before leveling off in subsequent years (Education Daily, 1984).

The U.S. Supreme Court's landmark decision regarding bilingual education was *Lau v. Nichols* in 1974. It helped spur the expansion of bilingual education in the United States. The Court concluded that "There is no equality of treatment merely by providing students with the same facilities, textbooks, teachers and curriculum." The May 25, 1970 memorandum issued by the U.S. Office of Civil Rights had already specified that a school program should be offered to children with limited English skills that provides them an opportunity to learn. (Fed. Reg. 1970). The Equal Education Opportunities Act of 1974, enacted by Congress in response to the *Lau* decision stated:

No state shall deny equal educational opportunity to an individual on account of his or her race, color, sex, or native origin, by the failure of an educational agency to overcome language barriers that impede equal participation by its students in its instructional progress. (Section 1703f)

The *Lau* decision also led Congrees to amend and broaden in 1974 the impact of the Bilingual Education Act of 1968. English speaking children were invited to participate in bilingual classes. In 1978, a second amendment mandated parental involvement and allowed English proficient students to form up to 40 percent of the class (Grosjean, 1975).

Aspira vs. the Board of Education of the City of New York resulted in a "Consent Decree" which gave school boards in the city legal support for initiating, structuring and implementing programs using the native language of the children as well as English. Since the *ASPIRA* decision was geared toward meeting the needs of Hispanic students in New York City, other ethnic language groups, including Greek Americans, met with the Chancellor of the New York City Board of Education and demanded bilingual program opportunities for their ethnic group's limited English speaking population. As a result of the meeting, Special Circular #114 was issued on June 26, 1975. However, this directive was largely ignored as the U.S. Office of Civil Rights noted after its site-visit in the summer of 1977. In the Fall of 1977, a "Lau Plan" was formulated by the New York City Board of Education which incorporated the education rights for Hispanic students entailed in the *ASPIRA Consent Decree* for all children in New York City whose native language was not English (Anemoyanis, 1980; Gimondo, 1982).

The public school bilingual education programs which are supported through federal funding are mostly "transitional" or, in other words, compensatory in nature. The programs are geared toward shifting from the use of the student's native language in the classroom to English only during a period of two or three years (Fishman, 1976). These LEP students in transitional bilingual education programs are then placed in mainstream classrooms with native English speaking students once they have attained a certain proficiency in English as measured, in New York City, by the Language Assessment Battery (LAB) (Chancellor's Report, 1987).

Misconceptions About Greek Bilingual Education
in the Public Schools

In spite of the fact that the federal legislation governing bilingual education, Public Law 98-511, Title VII, has the paramount goal of Americanization, i.e., the programs are not aimed at fostering the native language in and of itself but instead use the native language only as a "bridge" to English language development, many individuals and groups continue to view bilingual education as something "un-American," a threat to the cohesiveness and stability of American society

(Grosjean, 1985). As a result, the form of bilingual education which evolved treated the minority language "as a disease of the poor, . . . to be attacked by the disease baccilus itself. A little bit of deadened mother tongue, introduced in slow stages in the classroom environment, will ultimately enable the patient to throw off the mother tongue entirely and to embrace all-American vim, vigor, and vitality" (Fishman, 1976, p. 34).

At present, according to Cummins (1979), the "quick-exit" transitional bilingual approach which characterizes most public bilingual education programs is based on two fallacious and contradictory assumptions: "linguistic mismatch" and "maximum exposure." As Cummins states:

> On the one hand, based on the linguistic mismatch assumption, it is assumed that bilingual instruction in the early grades will be more effective in raising the level of English proficiency of minority students than instruction only through the medium of English. In other words, *less* time through the medium of English is assumed to result in greater development of English. Yet, it is simultaneously assumed that children must be exited from the bilingual program as rapidly as possible on the grounds that acquisition of English required maximum exposure to the language.

The "quick-exit" model of bilingual education ignores the body of research which indicates the positive effects of first language instruction over a longer period of time on the development of the second language and on the cognitive/academic development of the student. The transfer of skills between the first and second languages occurs because there is a "common underlying proficiency" which, as Cummins (1984) notes, ". . . implies that experience with *either* language can promote development of the proficiency underlying both languages, given adequate motivation and exposure to both either in school or in the wider environment" (p. 143).

Hence, if the first language of the student reaches only the level that Cummins (1979) terms BICS (Basic Interpersonal Communication Skills) and is not fully developed to the extent of what Cummins terms CALP (Cognitive/Academic Language Proficiency), then the result is what has been termed "subtractive bilingualism" by Lambert (1980).

This result leads the student to view his or her native language as inferior and to develop a negative attitude toward and only partial fluency in the second language. It is thus a more pedagogically sound practice to utilize an "additive bilingualism" approach wherein the student's native language proficiency is fully cultivated and the second language is introduced in a motivating manner (Cummins, 1980; Hakuta, 1986; Spiridakis and Sinatra, 1984).

It is also important to recognize that mere exposure to a second language is not enough, in and of itself, to develop language proficiency. Language learning episodes in the classroom should take into account the social contexts, motivation and attitudes of the target population, as well as the learning styles of the student (Spiridakis, 1981). The importance for teachers to incorporate appropriate instructional methods cannot be stressed enough. Language learning will not take place in a classroom atmosphere where the mode of instruction is purely "transmission-oriented," i.e., students are relegated to a role of participants who are expected to passively acquire bits of linguistic data. Research indicates the need for an active "reciprocal-interaction" classroom language learning approach which maximizes student interactions with the teacher and with one another (Cummins, 1984, Graves, 1983).

In the mid-1970's, as the Greek bilingual program was developing in New York City, a strong reaction was evoked in the large Greek American community. Greek American parents and educators were sharply divided over the issue of whether federally funded bilingual education was warranted for children of their ethnic group. A storm of protest accompanied what many Greek American parents living in an area with the highest concentration of Greeks outside of Greece, New York City, felt was the emergence of a program that would "mark" Greek children as socioeconomically inferior and would harm Greek speaking LEP children who needed only a little time to "catch on" in the regular monolingual English school program.

In spite of pressures from the Greek Americans in the community, in order to meet the needs of Greek LEP children, Community School District 30, which had 2,000 LEP students in 1974, hired an administrator to obtain funding for programs for all the LEP children in the district, including several hundred Greek LEP children in 1974. (Anemoyanis, 1982). Today the district has approximately 3,500 LEP students with about three hundred Greek LEP students enrolled in Greek bilingual education classes (NYC Board of Education, 1987).

Greek parental involvement and input was part and parcel of all such bilingual programs, and the District 30 program was no exception. However, certain parents in the district who feared that immigrant parents of children placed in the bilingual program had not been adequately informed as to the nature of the program, demanded at school board meetings that the schools be required to obtain the consent of parents prior to their child's participation in the program. This consent became a requirement for all bilingual programs in New York City public schools. Those parents who lobbied effectively against bilingual education, however, were, for the most part, against bilingual education as an educational treatment. Their voice was not the voice of the immigrant parents for the most part, who were not yet politically involved in the school process; but their activism served to reinforce and mirror the resentment and doubt that many principals had for the bilingual program. Moreover, the non-bilingual school personnel were incited against newly-hired bilingual teachers who were given jobs at a time when thousands of monolingual teachers in New York City were losing their positions due to stunning budget cuts (Gimondo, 1982).

Decentralization gave local community school districts and communities more control over the education of their students; but the outcries which occurred, especially in District 30, served to fuel gross misconceptions about, and animosity toward, bilingual education programs among Greek American parents and even Greek American educators and administrators. The result was a chilling effect on the full implementation of the programs throughout the district.

An amalgam of anti-Greek bilingual education sentiments were expressed in the Greek press and at school board meetings during the initial years of public Greek bilingual education. Many of the board members of the Greek parochial schools, as well as other administrators and personnel associated with these schools viewed the emergence of the public Greek bilingual education program as a threat to the stability and integrity of their schools which were viewed as the only agencies which could combine the transmitting of Greek language and heritage and still effectively Americanize Greek American children. The polemical attitude against Greek and other bilingual education programs betrayed a misunderstanding of the pedagogical goals of the public school programs and a sorely misguided rivalry, to say the least. For bilingual educators who recognized the role of bilingual education, the emergence of the public school program revealed, in effect, the need to serve a different population, for the most part, than the parochial schools served: the first generation immigrant Greek American child who spoke little or no English. While some of the parochial schools had tried to accommodate this population of LEP children, with some ESL instruction, provided usually with support services from the New York City Board of Education (which have recently terminated due to a Supreme Court ruling) the parochial schools were simply not geared toward serving these LEP children.

The hostility certain parochial school administrators and board members exhibit toward the public school bilingual program and, to a lesser extent, public schools in general, has recurred in recent years. The hostility, which sometimes takes the form of spreading negative rumors about the public school bilingual program and its personnel, is caused by the loss of potential students and teachers who, usually primarily for economic reasons, opt for or transfer to the public school system which has no tuition requirement and offers a substantially higher salary and benefits.

Acknowledgement by those involved in the administration and support of the parochial schools of the distinctly different and beneficial goals of the public bilingual education program was not forthcoming until several years later. The advent of research, writings and conferences featuring the goals and achievements of both programs gave rise to a better understanding between Greek American educators, administrators and parents involved in both school systems. In addition, many Greek American educators received in-service and pre-service training in bilingual education which clarified the need for, and role of, Greek bilingual education. Moreover, by 1980, the Greek Press in New York City had begun to run articles which emphasized the positive benefits and possibilities of bilingual education in the public and parochial schools (Spiridakis, 1987).

Greek Language Component Issues of the Parochial or
Private School System

There are approximately 3,500 students in New York City enrolled in the day parochial schools including two high schools and eleven elementary schools. Another 1,500 students attend the afternoon schools affiliated with the Archdiocese related Greek Orthodox Churches while another 700 students attend afternoon schools sponsored by Greek Orthodox Churches and a private school in Brooklyn.

As Fishman (1985) remarks on the subject of ethnic language education in the parochial schools:

> As though these schools benefit from the selfless dedication of thousands of parent/teacher activists, these schools are even more meager language-maintenance auxiliary agencies than they might or could optimally be . . . Rather than being instruments of language maintenance in any conscious, focused and determined fashion, ethnic community mother tongue schools are far more commonly instruments for combining both ethnicity and controlled mainstream exposure. (p. 375)

A curriculum guide for Greek language and cultural study is issued by the Education Department of the Archdiocese (1975). However, an inspection of this guide reveals its inappropriateness for learners of Greek as a second language, by and large. Hence, it is not surprising that most teachers of Greek find its usefulness mainly in areas unrelated to language such as history, social studies and religion. The Greek language component of the day schools as well as the afternoon schools should have a thoroughly prepared, common, systematic curriculum which subsumes an appropriate Greek as a second language methodology. There is also no uniform system of program evaluation to help teachers and administrators ascertain what language teaching methods are effective and to what extent, for example.

A promising note from a recent survey of parochial schools in New York City, is that the Greek teachers are shifting from use of traditional instructional strategies to modern ones (Spiridakis, 1987). It must be kept in mind that the personnel who staff the Greek component of the parochial schools and afternoon schools were mostly teachers trained in Greece and whose skills were limited to teaching Greek as a first language to native Greek speaking children. Since many parochial school children had surface level proficiency in Greek, or BICS in the language, these teachers, and their administrators, erroneously believed that the first or native language teaching strategies would work with these Greek American students. However, many of the Greek teaching staff today recognize the need to incorporate second language teaching methodology in the teaching of Greek. In addition, an increasing number of students enter the parochial programs with little or no speaking ability in Greek, which makes it all the more difficult to try to use first language teaching techniques. However, because of limited administrative financial and personnel resources, the textbooks and curricula for Greek language development are still at odds with the desired objective of bilingualism, in as much as the students often express frustration and even abandon these programs (Massialas, 1984; Spiridakis, 1978).

While both the public Greek bilingual and day parochial school programs utilize both the Greek and English languages in the curriculum, at the present time they are still, generally, utilized for different purposes. The general model of the day parochial programs can be termed an "enrichment-model." The student is learning a second language, (even though many Greek American children are raised speaking Greek) a minority-language, through Greek language-arts, culture and history. In the public school, the Greek language forms the basis of academic content instruction while the Greek-speaking LEP students receives English as a second language instruction. According to the generally used model, instruction in academic subjects is gradually shifted to English. Translation from English to Greek is used in most public school bilingual program classrooms. The outcome sought in the usual public Greek bilingual program is proficiency in English and an avoidance of the student falling behind in subject matters. A positive self-image is also a stated outcome in many such programs which recognize that use of the native language can enhance feelings of self-worth as the student learns academic subject in his or her mother tongue while learning English as a second language (Office of Bilingual Education, 1982).

In the parochial school realm, the desired outcomes are

the addition of Greek language and biculturalism to the student's repertoire of academic skills developed in English. However, because the Greek teaching personnel often employ methods and materials which are not "on par" with those of the English language curriculum, and because it is easy to see that fewer resources are invested in the Greek language curriculum, insofar as staffing, materials and curriculum, the student often develops ambivalent or even negative attitudes toward the Greek curriculum, the Greek teacher, and, to a lesser extent, perhaps, the Greek language itself (Spiridakis, 1978). In addition, the enhancement of student self-concept which has been the subject of research in Greek bilingual education, is an overlooked goal in the Greek parochial school curriculum which warrants inclusion (Flouris, Coulopoulos, & Spiridakis, 1981).

Public and Parochial Bilingual Education: Mastering the Possibilities

The two Greek Bilingual programs, public and parochial, begin to converge when one analyzes the bilingual development trends and the possibilities inherent in both curricula.

Today, in District 30, the Greek language has made its way into the curriculum of the regular monolingual English elementary program as a result of community activism and encouragement from New York State legislators who have joined Congress in once again recognizing and addressing the need to develop bilingual citizens through FLES (Foreign Language in the Elementary School) programs. At the same time, Greek parochial schools are introducing more English as a second language activities for LEP students enrolled.

Recognition of the positive cognitive benefits of bilingualism, not to mention sensitivity to avoiding embarrassing moments in the international sphere by politicians who display rampant ignorance of foreign languages and cultures at times, has steered New York State legislators to support public bilingual education which utilizes a "maintenance" approach which is more in line with the current research on immersion programs. The "Two-Way bilingual programs," developed and supported by the New York State Education Department, are structured so that EP youngsters and LEP children learn each other's languages in an educational environment conducive to developing full bilingualism in both groups of children. The programs, instituted in 1985, focus on the early childhood years and seek to utilize approaches, methods and materials which reflect the efficacy of the very latest research in these areas of education. However, these programs, including the pilot Two-Way program in District 30 for Greek children, suffer from a recurring problem associated with innovative programs. Federal, or in this case, State funds are allocated for use but the local administrators often choose not to commit, or are unable to identify and place, the most qualified personnel to staff the program; the effect is to hinder early program success (Spiridakis, 1987).

By the same token, the parochial schools, including the Education office of the Greek Orthodox Archdiocese of North and South America, in New York City, have, during the past several years drawn upon the research developments in applied linguistics, bilingual education and second language learning to improve the instructional strategies employed by Greek teaching personnel and to improve the quality of the curriculum and textbooks for Greek as well. The Education Department of the Archdiocese has sponsored many workshops in this effort for both day and afternoon school teachers. The Greek parochial school teachers and administrators have become more cognizant of the techniques of second language instruction, including the important role of attitudes, and have individually tried to develop curricula and methodology suitable for their group of students. In addition, but to a much lesser extent, some schools better serve the occasional LEP student who enrolls by drawing upon appropriate ESL methods and materials, including "Sheltered-English," which may be effective for certain Greek LEP children. Sheltered English focuses on simplified English language input and on meaning and function rather than grammar and pronunciation (Krashen, 1982, 1984). However, responsibility for such instruction is usually left to the individual teacher who may, without guidance from the principal, have attained competence in ESL instructional methodology which he or she uses to individualize instruction for a LEP student.

English proficient Greek Americans learning Greek in the parochial schools need "reciprocal-interaction" approaches which take the boredom out of second language learning. These children who are already proficient in the "majority" language of American society, can develop full proficiency in the Greek language if the proper planning, methods and materials are provided. These schools have the potential to incorporate into their curriculum to a larger extent the techniques associated with "immersion" language approaches, wherein more time can be spent teaching academic subjects in the Greek language rather than simply teaching the Greek language as a subject (Genesse, 1985; Lambert, 1984).

The parents of children enrolled in Greek bilingual programs in public and parochial school programs also must understand the possibilities, including enhanced cognitive skills and cognitive flexibility, associated with the developing research-based language policies and shaping Greek language curricula to reflect those policies (Hakuta, 1984). But parents and educators must realize that as Genessee notes, "High levels of proficiency in the bilingual's two languages are necessary to incur the positive cognitive effects that are associated with bilingualism (1985, p. 554).

Parental involvement in terms of their influence and attitudes toward bilingualism and second language learning can also impart significantly on school personnel and on their own children's attitudes toward language learning. Insofar as the parochial school systems are concerned, parents must recognize that the schools are competing with intense forces of Americanization and de-ethnicization which tend to trivialize the benefit of being a bilingual citizen (Fishman, 1980). Approaches which seek more effective language learning should be embraced, as they represent the potential for these schools to save a vital national resource. Greek parents desirous that their children excel in the mainstream of American society should not fear that more Greek instruction through viable and tested "immersion" approaches will endanger their children's Americanization.

By the same token, parents of children in the public school bilingual programs must communicate their desires to preserve the ethnic language through educational practices grounded in the aforementioned research. It is patently contradictory for policy-makers to espouse the desire to cultivate the foreign languages capabilities of our students and at the same time promote bilingual programs which are not structured for optimal learning and the development of bilingual proficiency.

To a large extent, the school boards of both the public and parochial school bilingual education systems bear the candle and snuffer of the future of the continued evolution and success of these programs, within given financial constraints. Principals also play a key role in shaping the programs through their attitudes and degree of support. The shroud of political considerations which dominate most boards has hampered the efforts of Greek American educators who have gained knowledge of the potentialities of parochial and public sectors. The time has come to allow Greek American educators with vision and courage, as well as expertise, to shape the language curricula. Communication of the possibilities, based on research rather than politics, is needed. The current political interests developing bilingualism provides the stage for enlightening board members, principals and other key personnel to recognize and apply the program models, approaches, methods and techniques which will work to reach the common goal of bilingualism and enhanced overall educational opportunities for all children.

The public Greek bilingual program in New York City's Community District 30 has been a battle field in the past, with lingering attacks coming from Greek Americans who are responding to popular alarmist notions regarding bilingual education. The "English Only" movement and related initiatives certainly confound the efforts of bilingual educators to preserve our resource of ethnic languages. Today, the support for Greek public bilingual programs appears to prevail in District 30. However, disconcerting violations of the "Lau Plan" still exist throughout the city and district. This phenomenon illustrates the degree to which certain parents and principals, as well as supervisors and board members, can exert their power and impose their view of what the education of LEP children should be, even if it violates their right to equal educational opportunity as denoted by the law. Steps need to be taken to remedy this situation, but a "grass-roots" community activism is needed to prod the appropriate agencies and administrators to act.

As for the parochial school system, an effort is long overdue to revamp the Greek curricula. While the public school programs have elaborate, systematic evaluation models in place, due to the availability of funds for this purpose, there is no systematic evaluation of the Greek language components of the parochial schools (See Orfanos & Tsemberis in Chapter 11). In addition, the parochial schools associated with the Archdiocese churches receive minimal technical assistance from the Education Department of the Archdiocese which has a staff of two. Funds and personnel are needed to bolster this department. However, the parochial school system offers its board and administrators greater autonomy over curriculum planning and programming than the public school in many respects. The offering of the Greek language is an integral part of the curriculum and represents what the public schools have been unable, until recently to a limited extent, to offer to the ethnic language community in terms of language "enrichment" education (Spiridakis, 1986).

Cross-fertilization of the ideas of educators and researchers in the public bilingual education areas and parochial school programs could generate innovative Greek immersion programs in the parochial day schools. This will never happen, of course, without a community-wide awareness of this form of bilingual education and the benefits which attend it. At the same time, public Greek bilingual programs could some day represent a native language approach which operates for the number of years necessary for the student to become a true bilingual with a positive attitude toward both English and the Greek language.

The prophetic words of Fishman (1976) over ten years ago remain poignant and meaningful for Greek bilingual education today:

> The school can provide instructional power for bilingual education but not the functional power for it. The latter must be provided by the community in terms of dignifying its own diversity or the diversity of the international community . . . (p. 111)

> . . . real bilingual education is not a political ploy. It is an educational advance. Our country has advanced and improved in many ways since the times of our (grand-) parents. Bilingual education is both old and new, both in the U.S.A. and throughout the world . . . It is now coming into its own in the U.S.A., and it is about time that it do so. It is the kind of 'special handling' that we *all* deserve, and that we will *all* benefit from. (p. 121)

REFERENCES

Anemoyanis, V. (1982). Greek bilingual education in historical perspective." In H. J. Psomiades and A. Scourby (Eds.), *The Greek American community in transitios* (pp. 171-180). New York: Pella.

Constantakos, C. M. (1982). Ethnic language as a variable in subcultural continuity. In H. J. Psomiades, and A. Scourby (Eds.), *The Greek-American community in transition* (pp. 137-170). New York: Pella.

Cummins, J. (1979). Linguistic interdependence and the educational development of bilingual children. *Review of Educational Research, 49*, 222-251.

Cummins, J. (1980). The entry and exit fallacy in bilingual education. *NABE Joursal, 4*, 25-29.

Cummins, J. (1984). *Bilingualism and special education: Issues in assessment and pedagogy*. San Diego: College-Hill Press, 1984.

Department of Education. (1975). *Objectives of The Greek American community school*. New York: Greek Orthodox Archdiocese of North and South America.

Education Daily. (1984, October 23).

Equal Education Opportunities Act (1974), 20 U.S.C. Section 1703(f). Federal Register 11595 (1970).

Fishman, J. A. (1976). *Bilingual education: An international sociological perspective*, Rowley, Ma. Newbury House.

Fishman, J. A. (1980). "Ethnocultural dimensions in the acquisition and retention of biliteracy. *Basic Writing, 3*, 48-61.

Fishman, J. A. et al. (1985). *The rise and fall of the ethnic revival*. New York; Mouton Publishers.

Flouris, G., Coulopoulos, D. and Spiridakis, J. (1981). *The self-concept of children. A guide for parents and teachers*. Athens: Orosimo Press.

Gimondo, A. (1982). Bilingual education: The New York experience. In J. Spiridakis and Stavropoulos, (Eds.), [Current perspectives on bilingual education] (pp. 19-24). *Impact*, 17.

Genessee, F. (1985). Second language learning through immersion. *Review of Educational Research, 55*, 541-561.

Graves, D. H. (1983). *Writing: Teachers and children at work*. Exeter, New Hampshire: Heinemann.

Grosjean, F. (1982). *Life with two languages*. Boston: Harvard University Press.

Hakuta, K. (1986). *Mirror of language: The debate of bilingualism*. New York: Basic Books.

Krashen, S. D. (1982). *Principles and practice in second language acquisition*. Oxford: Pergamon.

Krashen, S. D. (1984). Immersion: Why it works and what it has taught us. *Language and Society*, (Winter), 61-64.

Lambert, W. (1984). An overview of issues in immersion education. In *Studies on immersion education: A collection for the United States*. Sacramento, Ca., California State Department of Education.

Lau v. Nichols, 414 U.S. 563 (1974).

90   EDUCATION AND GREEK AMERICANS

Massialas, B. G. (1984). The education of Hellenes in Amercia: From melting pot to cultural pluralism. *The Ahepan*, (Fall), 22-24.

New York City Board of Education. (1987). *Answers to frequently asked questions about Limited English Proficient students and Bilingual/ ESL programs, 1985-1986*. Office of Bilingual Education.

Ovando, C. J. and Collier, V. P. (1985). *Bilingual and ESL classrooms*. New York: McGraw Hill.

Program evaluation of Community School District 19 Two-Way Bilingual Education Program, 1985-86. (1986, October). Unpublished Manuscript. Office of Bilingual Education, New York City Board of Education.

Ramirez, A. G. (1985). *Bilingualism through schooling* Albany, State University of New York.

Saloutos, Theodore. (1964). *The Greeks in the United States*. Cambridge, Ma., Harvard University Press.

Schneider, S. (1976). *Revolution, reaction or reform* New York: Las Americas.

Spiridakis, J. (1987, June). Greek Bilingual Education: The future of the Greek language. Paper presented to the Tenth Annual New York State Bilingual Educators Conference. New York City.

Spiridakis, J. Diagnosing and prescribing instruction based on the learning styles of bilingual students. In R. V. Padilla, (Ed.) *Ethnoperspectives in Bilingual Education: Vol. III*. Eastern Michigan University.

Spiridakis, J. (1978). *The effects of Greek cultural units drawn from the popular arts on the attitudes toward, and knowledge of, the Greek culture*. Unpublished doctoral dissertation, Florida State University, Florida.

Spiridakis, J. and Sinatra, R. (1984). Sociocultural foundations of reading for bilingual children. In A. L. Carrasquillo asd P. Segan (Eds.), *The teaching of reading in Spanish to the bilingual student*. Madrid: Ediciones Alcala.

Waggoner, D. (1980). European language minorities of other than Spanish in the United States. Paper presented to the Ninth Annual International Bilingual Bicultural Education Conference, Anaheim, Ca.

CHAPTER 5

GREECE AND GREEK AMERICA: THE FUTURE OF THE GREEK AMERICAN COMMUNITY

HARRY J. PSOMIADES

The purpose of this paper is to make a few observations about the future of Greek America. I would like to suggest to the reader and particularly to our leadership and that of Greece the course that must be taken if we are to survive as a community. Much has been written on the subject of Hellenic ethnic identity in the United States; but my impression is that this literature, for the most part, has not been read, nor has it been fully understood. It is unfortunate because the next two or three decades will determine whether or not we will ultimately succumb to the white death of assimilation demanded by the assimilationists or to the darkness of an ever shrinking ghetto demanded by the equally chauvinistic separatists. They will also determine whether or not we move toward a more pluralist integration in American society in which the validity of a common culture, to which all individuals have access, is upheld, while sustaining and enhancing our own integrity and ethnic nuclei. Whether or not we will stay our course and avoid the Scylla of assimilation as well as the Charybdis of a ghetto existence will depend upon a sensitized and farsighted Greek American and Greek leadership as well as upon the incessant labor, sacrifice and insight of all our communities across America (Psomiades, 1984).

The Nature of the Greek American Community

While the goal of pluralist integration in contrast to the integrationist model will not eliminate ethnic boundaries, neither will it maintain them intact (Higham, 1974). No ethnic group can have or rely upon the support of the general community in strengthening its boundaries, all ethnic boundaries are understood to be permeable. Yet, within these boundaries the core of ethnicity is respected as an enduring center of social action. This dual commitment to a general culture and an ethnic nucleus requires that we reject the superficiality and chauvinism of assimilation as well as the parochialism of ethnocentrism. It requires, if I may paraphrase Michael Novak (1975), the development of a multicultural consciousness and a pluralistic personality which recognizes its own rootage, draws consciously from its own resources, and tries to become skilled both in self-knowledge and in the accurate perception and understanding of those with different roots.

There are according to Charles C. Moscos (1980) two competing versions of the Greek experience in America. One is that Greek Americans are part of a homeland extension, an homogenia, an Hellenic diaspora. The other is that Greek Americans are entrants and then participants in American history. The difference between the two views are of course exaggerated and each contains part of the truth. It is clear that as members of a diaspora we cannot be immune to the environment in which we find ourselves. As ethnic Americans we cannot be indifferent to the realities of Greece and our Greek immigrant cultural heritage. Yet, at least for those born in the United States and certainly for the third and fourth generations of Greek Americans one's identity is not so much that of a member of a diaspora, a transplanted Greek, but rather that of the sensibility of an American ethnic. While the two views may exist together for some time in cities such as New York, with large recent Greek immigrant populations, it is clear that in time the view that Greek Americans must be placed in the broad context of the ethnic experience in America is *more* valid than the diaspora perspective. Indeed, the bulk of Greek Americans, those beyond the first generation, look at the world scene and happenings in Greece more from the perspective of Americans than of Greeks. As the late historian of Greek America, Theodore Saloutos (1980), reminded us, it would be unrealistic to expect them to react otherwise. Not only because they were born, educated, and formed their basic philosophy of life in the United States, but also because in their formative years there had been little if any contact with Greece. We should not forget that their parents and grandparents came to America either as refugees or from the villages and towns of Greece which could not sustain them. They were a surplus population which made a conscious and free choice to immigrate and to adopt a new land as their own. This is often overlooked among Greeks here or recent arrivals to the United States who often denounce the Greek Americans as unGreek and hurt whatever justifiable expectation they might have had for support from Greek Americans.

Yet, while we have fully entered American society, we have maintained strong communal ties and a profound consciousness of ethnic identiy and heritage, as every poll or study of Greek Americans has substantiated (Gallup, 1980). For the most part we are a people with strong affection for the land of our forefathers; and in our deepest inclination of conduct, religious approach, social bias, feeling for family, we continue to maintain the heavy influences of the original Greek immigrant culture. There has been a persistent attachment to "Greek identity" well into the second and third generation (Moskos, 1980). For most of us Greek ethnic identity has been a badge to be worn proudly or a way of life to be personally treasured, though not made a public issue. For some it has been incidental, or a curiosity, and for an unfortunate few it has been a stigma to be forgotten or evaded as much as possible.

The first Greek immigrants, illiterate and impoverished, through hard work, great personal sacrifice, and an awesome dedication built our churches and social institutions and provided the support and encouragement required for the education of their children. In time, the institutions the immigrants created and the values which they cherished had to adapt to an increasingly tolerant American environment. Moreover, their children had entered the American middle-class. Thus, as a community they could no longer remain simply a pale reflection of an old country culture. Indeed, Greek American ethnicity has acquired a dynamism of its own and must be taken and respected in its own right as part of the American subculture, which itself is a story of many different heritages and of the human spirit in its many guises (Sowell, 1980). The emergence of a Greek American sub-culture reflects the homogenization of American-born Greeks with regard to each other rather than their absorption into a the general American population (Moskos, 1980).

The Maintenance of the Greek American Community

Can we maintain and expand the boundaries of our Greek American sub-culture? Barring a major calamity, the days of massive Greek immigration to the New World are over. Moreover, mixed-marriages among Greek Americans will continue their upward spiral. Family structure, religion and social organization, which sustained the community in the past, are themselves facing major crisis both here and in Greece. Will our sub-culture nurture and sustain our children and those beyond or will the assimilationists and ghettoizers win out? Since the challenge is not unique to Greek Americans, we may well ask will all American sub-cultures ultimately end up in the dust bin of history? On the other hand there are positive points to consider, advantages which our parents did not have. As the recent census shows Greek Americans are not only better educated and wealthier than their parents but also more advanced than most American ethnic groups. Moveover, unlike previous generations of Greek Americans, we live in a society which has accepted for the time being at least the validity of cultural pluralism and one in which ethnicity has become a legitimate focus for group mobilization for political and economic ends. We also live at a time when the Greek state has apparently taken a greater interest in the Greek diaspora. We are not without resources in the task of defending and expanding ethnic boundaries.

A clue as to what is to be done may be found in a general investigation of interest groups. The reason that no interest group is safe, whether it be an ethnic group or not, is that the individual is a universe of interests, with a variety of concerns whose priorities change along with changes in the individual's life and fortune. To maintain his sanity, the individual must and does prioritize these concerns. Interest groups know this and to achieve a high priority status and maintain it they tend to exaggerate their importance in the individual's life. They attempt to capture the complete attention of the individual going beyond the immediate concern of the group. Thus, the approach for the survival of the group whether it be a trade union, a religious or ethnic group, or a businessman's association is multidimensional. To survive they may engage in a broad spectrum of activities: religious, social, recreational, educational, political and economic. A program for action in the Greek American community must also clearly recognize the need for flexibility. Our communities are complex aggregates of complex groups and individuals; our needs are not identical nor are the perceived challenges. We operate in different environments, in different social, economic and political contexts. We are confronted with the conflicting needs of different generations.

Courses of action to ensure the maintenance of our cultural heritage and identity include the following:

1.   In the broadest sense community survival depends on education and education begins at home. It is the parents who must supply the foundation upon which our educational system is based. If they do not do their job, the priests, professional educators and community leaders will be hard pressed to do theirs. We must as parents, reinforce our primary function, namely to bear and develop our children to the greatest extent possible. But the present trend in American life (with games, sports, and above all television and videos) has distracted us from our fundamental responsibility—to pass on our heritage, our culture, to our children. Not to do so fully is to defraud our own creations and to betray past generations.

2.   While it is true, as every ethnic group study shows, that the loss of ethnic language by the third generation does not necessarily mean the loss of community identity, it does mark the shrinkage of community boundaries or a contraction of community. While the loss of language is not the end of our Greek community life, it certainly is the beginning of the end of that life. Therefore, the community must supply the funds, organization and planning necessary for Greek language maintenance; and with the decline of Greek immigration, only the community can supply the motivation of our young to learn the language. Only the community, in its pluralist sense, and not as ghetto, can give our young a feeling of pride and ethnic awareness and thus provide a hospitable and congenial environment for the learning and use of Greek. In this regard we are fortunate that, unlike the past, our society no longer frowns upon the use of foreign languages.

Indeed, it is obligated under the Helsinki Accords to promote foreign language instruction in the United States. In short, we must ensure the teaching of modern Greek language, literature, history and culture, at all levels, from primary school to the university. We should also develop a system of inexpensive correspondence courses on a major scale in order to service isolated communities and individuals. Not only should our subject matter be introduced wherever possible in our public school system and in the texts it uses but we should also expand and support the Greek parochial and community day schools. They should, of course, be under the direction of professionals, employing the most effective teaching methods and materials. In all of our educational endeavors we must bar the way of the academic charlatan, the educational incompetent, and the political opportunist. We should try to establish at least two or three Greek American gymnasia or live-in prep schools with the highest standards in appropriate locations across America.

There is also the imperative that we radically modify our system, if one can call it that, of recruiting, training, and compensating our teachers. We certainly must pay our teachers much more if we expect intellectually capable and motivated men and women to choose the teaching of Greek and related subjects as a life's work and remain committed to it. University faculty in Greek Studies must accelerate their efforts to develop the discipline and at the same time must abandon traditional disdain for primary and secondary school teachers. We must do our share in nurturing among our teachers professional pride in subject matter. This involves ready access to research and meetings as well as opportunities to participate in a field and seek advancement and recognition within a discipline's professional community or association. Attachment to a subject can make a teacher, but enthusiasm for a subject can be sustained only by constant contact with the discipline. In this regard, seminars, conferences and intellectual exchanges among teachers are absolutely vital. It is regretable that it is only now in the long history of Greek America that a major conference has been held on the problems of education and our communties (Orfanos & Psomiades, 1986). Finally, teachers should be regularly recertified in their subject area and the community must extend to them the respect that is their due as professionals.

3. Perhaps most important for the maintenance of Greek

ethnicity is the voluntary participation of individuals in Greek American religious, social, professional and educational institutions. These institutions, whether they are the Greek Orthodox Church and its related or affiliated organizations, the *topika sommatia*, veterans organizations, professional and fraternal associations, the American Hellenic Educational Progressive Association (AHEPA) family, sports and cultural groups must be encouraged and supported. Clearly, if you do not belong to any of the above groups, you are on your way out of the community. In the long run, of course, if enough people drop out, the community itself is threatened with extinction.

4. Quality Greek American publications, radio, newspapers, journals and television programs in both Greek and English should be brought into the home on a regular basis. This is an essential component of the educational process that is all too often ignored.

5. Cultural and educational exchange programs between various Greek American communities, between the communities and Greece, and between the various Greek diasporas should be initiated or considerably expanded. The Israeli Jewish experience, with which we have much in common, would be a worthwhile model. Each year hundreds of Jews go to Israel to participate in cultural and educational programs. Unlike the Greek university system, their universities have shown greater foresight and flexibility in accommodating the non-native student. In this context we should also include meaningful contacts and exchanges between various leadership groups. We should also include university exchanges, particularly exchange programs between various Greek studies centers in the United States and Greek universities and research centers.

6. Greater efforts should be made to identify, recruit, and support potential leaders in the community. And in the larger society in which we live we should continue to blend the Greek lore of political battle with the American tradition of public service. It would be beneficial both to the nation and the community. I would also like to remind the reader that our battle is here and not in Greece. The new immigrant must register, must vote, and must get involved in American politics in all of its aspects and not simply on Greek issues. We must get involved in the on-going task of creating and supporting permanent institutions of community and not expend our

energies as partisans of Athenian politics. Those of you familiar with the history of the Greek American community know all too well of the near destruction of the community resulting from the conflict between Venizelists and Constantinists which spilt over from Greece into the United States during the inter-war years.

The community must also make sophisticated and careful decisions about candidates of Greek ancestry who ask for our support. Peter Marudas (1982), the very talented aide to Senator Paul Sarbanes, reminds us that it is not merely a potential candidate's Greek background that should guarantee automatic support, but qualities consistent with high political standards. It is the community's responsibility to exercise careful scrutiny of prospective candidates lest it foolishly squander political resources and/or its decision becomes a source of embarrassment.

Finally, all of the above require money, organization, management skills, a sense of the possible and careful planning. They require the setting up of meaningful priorities because we live and will always live in a world of scarcity. There will never be enough money or talent to do all that must be done. At the same time, whatever action we as a community take should not in any way restrain or discourage individual initiatives. In the final analysis if we succeed as community into the fifth and sixth generation, it will depend as it has in the past primarily upon individual initiatives—the choir director, the individual parish priest, the sports director, the lonely editor, the dedicated teacher, an inspired parent, an officer or member of an association or club. Indeed, it will depend, as in the past, on the hundreds of unsung heroes who have done so much without recognition. Yet, the organized community and Greece should not be taken "off the hook." They have not done what they should have done particularly in the field of education, they have not done as well as they could have done. If I were to grade them I would give them a charitable "C."

Greece and Greek America: Harmony or Discord?

Both Greece and Greek America have a common goal; namely, the preservation and development of a Greek cultural identity in the United States. Nevertheless, the potential for discord is also present, threatening the very goals both wish to achieve and our ability to do those things which must be done for our ethnic survival. It is therefore necessary that we attempt to understand the roots of this potential for discord:

1. What kind of Greek cultural identity is to be preserved? Is this culture to be a rubber stamp of the changing culture of Greece; or is it to be an American sub-culture drawing from its American environment, its old immigrant values, and from the evolving culture of modern Greece. The vast majority of Greek Americans are not simply transplanted Greeks, although a minority are. For the most part Greece and Greeks have not come to terms with this reality. It is beyond their historical experience, an experience in which the Greek immigrant or colonist brought with him a culture "superior" to the one he found in his new environment. This misunderstanding often creates friction between Greek Americans and new immigrants as well as between Greek American and Greek political elites.

2. What are the appropriate roles of the Greek Orthodox Church and the Greek state in Greek America? Between these two institutions there is, unavoidably perhaps, a natural potential of rivalry and tension over the "leadership" of the Greek American community. Historically, as we all know, it was the Greek Orthodox Church which served as the focus of community and provided the cement which bound us together (Patrinacos, 1982). To a large extent, it continues to provide this function. On the other hand, the Greek state hardly played a role in the evolving Greek American community. It was either too weak, preoccupied with more important issues, or indifferent. It only became aware of Greek America in a meaningful way after World War II, that is some fifty years after the first major wave of Greek immigrants reached these shores.

3. There is a tendency of the Greek state to disregard the autonomy of the Greek Church in America and to believe that it is dealing with the Greek community or diaspora rather than with a Greek American community. It is natural, that in a conflict between a state and its diaspora, the state will attempt to demand obedience. But as we have emphasized the Greek American community is not a Greek diaspora, as that term is traditionally understood, but is an American and for the most part a Greek Orthodox sub-culture with clearly a

great deal of love, affection and goodwill toward the once motherland.

4.   Greek politicians and recent Greek immigrants have a tendency to import the political battles of Greece and impose them on the community. As a community, we are naturally interested in a free and democratic Greece and we are concerned with its territorial integrity, but beyond that what goes on in Greece is basically not our affair and should in no way interfere with our quest to establish permanent and vibrant institutions and to safeguard our culture and sense of community for future generations.

5.   As the Greek American community evolved, new national, regional and local centers of influence within the community emerged beyond the control and direction of the Church and Greece. Varying in strength, they have developed their own networks of communication and mobilization. I have in mind the largest of such groups—AHEPA but also the various veterans, business, educational, and other professional and social organizations. This development was inevitable, reflecting a natural and dynamic evolution of a complex, diversified, upwardly mobile community. The leadership of these groups frequently find themselves in competition with one another, with the Church and Church affiliated leadership, and with the political elites of Greece. On occasion, regretfully, this healthy competition and disagreement leads to rivalry and tension at the price of our further development as community. It should be recognized that neither the Church nor Greece have a monopoly on the decisions affecting Greek America, although they have played or can play crucial roles in its development.

The Future of the Greek American Community

I do not believe that we will have a bright future, unless we are prepared, all of us, to enter into a serious, on-going, dialogue about the problems which confront us. And if it means showing our "dirty linen" or stepping on very sensitive toes, so be it. The dialogue must be a meaningful one and not simply put on for show. It must not be "controlled" or the monopoly of a single individual or group. We must all subordinate our personal differences, our vanity, and our quest for personal aggrandizement so that Hellenism may survive in the New World and enrich the lives of unborn generations.

In this encounter, we cannot dismiss Greece because for the Greek American sub-culture to survive as we move into the future we must maintain and develop further our ties with the Greek world. We cannot dismiss the Greek Orthodox Church because it is, perhaps, the most important or major component of our Greek American sub-culture and community life. Although many of our youth, including children of mixed marriages, do not speak Greek, they feel very much a part of the Greek American community because of their religion. There is a cultural persistence. The Church serves as much as a badge of ethnic identity as of religion.

We all know that what is needed to ensure our survival as a community is understanding by all parties concerned, planning, and perhaps most important to set our priorities so that we maximize the effectiveness of our resources, human as well as material. This has simply not happened. We evidently do not know what the term "priority" means. Our current definition of priority is given to those projects which, in the short run, give the largest visibility to the donor but are generally wasteful in the long run. Both Greece and Greek America share another cultural characteristic which has impeded our progress as community; namely, the reluctance to make meaningful judgments about programs and individuals. To set your priorities means to examine carefully and critically all projects and to assign to each project a place on your scale of priorities for the community based on need, merit and future viability.

Our experience in Greek Studies and higher education presents a good example. We are all in agreement that modern Greek Studies have a place in the curriculum of colleges and universities and that these centers or programs when fully developed will play a major role in community life and serve to strengthen the bonds between Greece and the United States. There are presently about a dozen centers or programs in various stages of development in California, Minnesota, Illinois, Ohio, Indiana, Florida, New Jersey, New York, and Massachusetts. They range from a one-man operation to full scale BA programs along with community out-reach programs and publications. But to date no meaningful attempt has been made by the community leadership and Greece to evaluate these programs in terms of their quality, university support, effectiveness, viability, growth potential, scope or range of activities, and financial need. When the time comes, all too infrequently, for the allocation of resources it is seldom based on the merits of the case.

In conclusion, despite the barriers we face, our pride and respect for our traditions will make our presence as visible in the future as it has been in the past. And after all, all of our institutions and progress have emerged from struggle. There is no reason to believe that the future will be any different.

REFERENCES

Gallup, G. (1980, October/November). Poll. *Orthodox Observer*.

Higham, J. (1974, July/August). Integration v. pluralism: An American dilemma. *The Center Magazine*.

Marudas, P. N. (1982). Greek American involvement in contemporary politics. In H. J. Psomiades & A. Scourby (Eds.), *The Greek American community in transition* (pp. 93-110). New York: Pella.

Moskos, C. C. (1980). *Greek Americans: Struggle and success*. Englewood Cliffs, NJ: Prentice-Hall.

Novak, M. (1975, May). On cultural ecology: The U.S. as nervous system of the planet's cultures. In R. Gambino (Ed.), *Ethnic studies* (p. vi) (a working paper). The Rockefeller Foundation.

Orfanos, S. D., & Psomiades, H. J. (Co-chairs). (1986, May). Conference on Education anl Greek Americans: Process and Prospects. New York.

Patrinacos, N. D. (1982). The role of the Church in the evolving Greek Americas community. In H. J. Psomiades & A. Scourby (Eds.), *The Greek American community in transition* (pp. 125-136). New York: Pella.

Psomiades, H. J. (1984). Contemporary Hellenism in the English-speaking world: Trends and prospects. In A. Farmakides, K. Kazazis, N. M. Vaporis, A. Anagnostopoulos, and H. J. Psomiades (Eds.), *The teaching of Modern Greek in the English-speaking world* (pp. 8-12). Brookline, Mass.: Hellenic College.

Saloutos, T. (1980, November 27). Greeks and Greek Americans-A need for better understanding. *The Hellenic Journal*, p. 2.

Sowell, T. (1980, December 4). Ethnic groups, prejudice and economic progress. *Wall Street Journal*, p. 30.

PART 2

EDUCATIONAL AND PSYCHOLOGICAL ISSUES

CHAPTER 6

PARENTAL INFLUENCE ON GREEK AMERICAN CHILDREN

JAMES R. CAMPBELL, CHARLENE CONNOLY
AND
LAWRENCE SVRCEK

The Greek American community has been one of the most successful at maintaining its identity amid the multicultural diversity of the United States. One of the prime reasons for this accomplishment has been the functioning of the many parochial schools that have been developed to serve this community. These schools have maintained the fundamental religious values of the group and have also transmitted much of the cultural heritage.

This study analyzed the influence that Greek American parents exerted on their children while attending Greek parochial schools. We tried to answer the following questions:

1. Does parental influence affect the math and reading achievement of elementary school children?

2. Do the parents provide the same influence to males and females?

3. Do the parents of emigrant children exert different kinds of influence than the parents of first generation or native born Americans?

4. Do parents within one parent families exert different kinds of influence than two parent families?

All of these questions can be subsumed within one broad question—How much of the children's success in school can be related to the influence of their parents?

PERSPECTIVE

Researchers have known for decades that parents are able to influence the achievement of their children (Coleman, 1966). However, few researchers expected that parental influence could account for 30 to 50 percent of the achievement variance. Yet, Marjorbanks (1979) and others have isolated a series of sociopsychological family variables that account for the high levels of variance. They have labeled these items press variables.

Our own study involves a different series of press variables that the parents of different ethnic groups use to influence math and reading achievement. We have isolated these press variables for Chinese American and Greek American parents so that we could tease out the cultural effects that intervene when these press variables are applied.

METHODS

The data for this study were derived from a three-part questionnaire—Inventory of Parental Influence (IPI). This instrument was initially developed from a qualitative study that used open-ended interviews with different groups of 5th and 6th grade children of varied ethnic backgrounds. The earlier version of the IPI contained 73 items and was administered to 751 students from very different ethnic backgrounds. Several factor analyses were performed to isolate the underlying factors. The most interpretable analysis (varimax rotation) produced five factors (alpha reliabilities ranged from .83 to .58).

The current version of the IPI (Form D56) contains 26 Likert items in Part I, 26 frequency items in Part II, and 12 demographic items in Part III. The test isolates four factors (13 items/factor) that have been labeled:

1. Parental Pressure
2. Parental Support/Expectations
3. Parental Helping
4. Parental Monitoring

The reader can get a better understanding of these factors

by examining some of the items included within each of the factors.

For the pressure factor, a high score is achieved if the student would agree or strongly agree with such statements as: I'm afraid to go home with a failing mark; when it comes to school my parents expect the impossible; my parents do not feel I'm doing my best in school. All of these items suggest a demanding parent that exerts pressure to retain high levels of performance. For the support factor, the student would agree or strongly agree with these statements: My parents are satisfied if I do my best; my parents want me to go to a "good" college; my parents are proud of me. These items suggest a supportive atmosphere at home. Parents that create such an atmosphere would appear to be attempting to develop a strong self-concept within their child.

The helping factor asks how often the parent would: go over my mistakes from a test; my parents help me with my schoolwork; my parents help me study before a test. The emphasis here, is upon the parents giving the time that is needed to actually help the child complete the school work. High scores for this factor would suggest fostering less independence for the child. The last factor requires agreeing with some statements and also indicating how often the child must do to the following: I'm expected to do my homework at the same time each night; my parents determine how much television I can watch; my parents make me watch "educational" television. Families with high scores in this area have distinct rules about homework, studying, T.V., and reading.

The demographic variables included in this study were gender, emigration status of the families (generation), family structure, and the educational level attained by the mother and father.

The achievement of the students was determined by utilizing the reading and mathematics scores obtained by the Metropolitan Achievement tests. These achievement tests were uniformly administered in all the Greek Parochial schools that participated in this study.

The full set of predictor and dependent variables that were used in this study were:

Predictor Variables	*Dependent Variables*
1. Gender	1. Reading Achievement
2. Family Structure	2. Math Achievement
3. Emigration	
4. Fathers Education	
5. Mothers Education	
6. Parental Pressure	
7. Parental Support/ Expectations	
8. Parental Helping	
9. Parental Monitoring	

In order to answer the first research question (determining the effect of parental influence on achievement) we calculated stepwise regression analyses. The first analysis used reading achievement as the dependent variables, the second analysis used mathematics achievement. Both analyses used 7 of the independent variables as predictors. (All but generation and family structure.)

The second research question involved gender comparisons. This question was investigated by calculating a series of analysis of variance (ANOVA) tests on 7 of the predictor variables and also on the two dependent variables.

The third research question involved the emigration status of the children's families. We attempted to get an answer to this question by calculating another set of ANOVA tests for the following groups:

1. Native born Americans: the students and both parents were born in the U.S.A.
2. First Generation Americans: the student was born in the U.S.A. but one or both parents were born overseas.
3. Emigrants: the student was born overseas and both parents were also born overseas.

The final research question involved an analysis of one and two parent families. To study this question we calculated another set of ANOVA tests by sorting the sample into the following groups:

1. One parent families due to the death of a parent.
2. One parent families due to divorce or separation.
3. Two parent families.

Data Source

The data for this study were derived by testing 4th, 5th and 6th grade children in two different Greek Parochial schools. The sample included 72 boys and 65 girls. Both schools were affiliated with Greek Orthodox churches and both were located in predominantly urban areas.

RESULTS

Achievement-Reading

The stepwise regression analysis uncovered one significant variable (F = 12.22, $p < .0007$) for reading achievement-parental pressure. This variable accounted for 10 percent of the reading variance. The correlation between children with high reading scores and parental pressure was r = −.311. The negative correlation indicates that those children that received lower levels of parental pressure compiled higher levels of reading achievement.

Achievement-Mathematics

This stepwise regression analysis uncovered one significant variable (F = 5.55, $p < .02$) for math achievement-parental monitoring. This variable accounted for 5% of the math variance but was also negatively correlated with achievement (r = −.215). The highest scoring math students were monitored less by their parents.

Gender Differences

There was only one significant difference between the boys and girls in this sample and this involved parental pressure. The boys received significantly more pressure than the girls (F = 7.415, $p < .007$). The boys also received more help from their parents but the difference did not reach significance, (F = 2.656, $p < .1055$). In terms of achievement the girls scored higher than the boys for both reading and mathematics but the differences did not reach significance.

Generation

The majority of children in this study were included in the first generation category (87%). Two variables were found to have significant differences (Educational level of fathers, Parental pressure). The native born American fathers had significantly higher levels of education ($F = 7.012$, $p < .01$). The native born American mothers also have higher levels of education that the mothers of the other groups, but the differences did not reach significance ($F = 2.416$, $p < .09$). Both of these findings point to the increased opportunity that is offered to emigrants in the United States. Such individuals are able to secure more education than they could in the foreign countries of their birth.

One parental factor was found to produce significant differences—parental pressure. The emigrant families exerted significantly more pressure than native born families ($F = 3.82$, $p < .02$). Surprisingly, the native born families supplied more monitoring than the emigrant families but the difference did not reach significance ($F = 1.604$, $p < .205$). Usually, high levels of pressure are accompanied by careful monitoring by the parents.

It is interesting to note that there were no significant differences for the reading and math achievement for the three groups of children. One would expect that the native born Americans would have much higher levels of reading achievement because the reading test was in the English language. Both the emigrant children and the children in the first generation group could be expected to be fluent in the Greek language and consequently have more trouble with a test conducted in English. Many of these children use English as a second language and this factor could be expected to penalize them in both achievement tests. Apparently, these Greek Parochial schools do an excellent job in teaching these children English.

Family Structure

Most of the families in this study (91 percent) were two parent families. There were very few one parent families at all. This would indicate that divorce and separation are not as common in Greek-American communities as they are in the rest of the U.S. society. There were no significant differences for any variables within these three family groupings. However there were some interesting differences to note. There were important differences between two parent families and one parent families with one deceased parent for the following: lower levels of reading achievement for the one parent families and higher levels of parental pressure, helping and monitoring. One can sense the increased demands that are made on the children within such families. The two parent families had higher achievement than both one parent families. These groups will be much more interesting to follow for other ethnic groups where there is more divorce and separation.

DISCUSSION

The larger question that we addressed in this study was— How much do parents influence their childrens' achievement in school? We limited our attention to the most fundamental areas, reading and mathematics.

If all of the different statistical tests are considered together with the findings of other studies done in the field, we can construct simplified causal models to help explain both kinds of achievement. Both models are speculative and will require much more research to confirm or reject. However, both models do combine a number of different variables and order them into a logical, easily understood pattern.

Both models include the education of the mother as an important variable. Two of our own studies have shown this variable to be important for high levels of achievement-especially in mathematics. (Campbell, Connolly & Pizzo, 1986a, 1986b). Welsh (1983) showed that for girls their mothers had a major influence on their values. Both models mediate the parents influence through gender. By this we mean that our different qualitative and quantitive studies have shown that the parents of all the cultures we have studied, socialize boys differently than girls. This study confirms this finding. For both math and reading achievement we found that parents pressure and monitor boys differently than girls.

Now let us analyze each of the models separately. The reading achievement model includes a bilingual element for

Greek American students. (See Figure 1). We have diagrammed the emigrant status of the family as directly related to both the parents influence and also to English as a second language variable. We feel that the sample used in this study was largely bilingual, and at least the emigrant subjects used English as a second language. (Perhaps a number of first generation students also use English as a second language). Such language deficiencies would certainly effect the reading achievement since the Metropolitan Reading test was limited to English.

The key area in the model involves the different parental variables. The family emigration status together with the education level of the mother both interact to produce a cultural orientation which in turn influences the parental factors. For this study Greek-American parents pressured and monitored boys more than girls. There are also many other variables that help contribute to reading achievement that we have not entered in this model. Perhaps different methods of teaching reading are involved, similarily different teacher variables might make a contribution and finally other socioeconomic status variables can be expected to have an effect. But our purpose was to simplify the findings and not to try and explain any general theory of reading achievement.

Our causal model for mathematics achievement includes some of the same variables that were placed in the reading model. (See Figure 2). There are two additional elements—Teachers, Independence/Autonomous learners.

The reader will note that one more parental factor is included in this model-parental helping. All three parental factors (pressure, monitoring and helping) were found to be negatively correlated with math achievement. We feel that parents encourage their children to become more independent by applying less pressure, by monitoring less and by not directly helping with their childrens' school work. The parents appear to be trying to develop autonomous learners. By this we mean children that will take responsibility for their own learning in math. Such qualities would be useful when the child takes difficult standardized math exams where much of the material is unfamiliar or new. Several other researchers have implicated autonomy as a critical variable for math achievement. (Fennema, 1984; Dweck, Davidson, Nelson, - Enna, 1978; Grant, 1983; Steinkamp & Maehr 1984).

The teacher's behavior has been included in the model

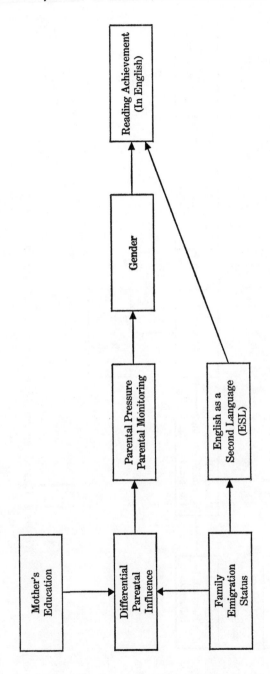

Figure 1. Causal relationships hypothesized for reading achievement.

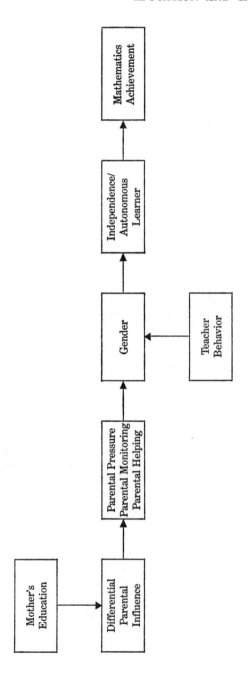

Figure 2. Causal relationships hypothesized for mathematics achievement.

because several different researchers have shown that elementary school teachers socialize boys differently than girls. (Brophy & Good, 1974; Grant, 1983, Stockard & Wood, 1984; Meece, 1984). Boys receive so much more criticism both for their behavior and also for their schoolwork that they tend to downplay the criticism. Instead, they develop their own ways of attacking math problems. This leads to a lot more autonomous learning on their part. Girls are socialized instead to be docile and compliant. (Grant, 1983, Dweck, et al. 1978). In our opinion the same socialization forces occur in the children's homes and therefore reinforce these teacher influences. Both the parents and the elementary teachers socialize the boys to develop the inner mechanisms which will eventually result in higher math achievement. For our own study the girls had higher levels of achievement mainly because they also had less pressure, less monitoring and less helping.

Again we would expect other researchers to add variables to the model as more and more information about math achievement is accumulated. Our purpose in presenting both achievement models is to stimulate research in this area.

REFERENCES

Brody, J. E., & Good, T. (1974). *Teacher-student relationships: Causes and consequences.* New York: Holt, Rhinehart, & Winston.

Campbell, J. R., & Connolly, C. (1984a). *Winners of the Westinghouse Talent Search.* Unpublished manuscript.

Campbell, J. R., & Connolly, C. (1984b). *Impace of ethnicity on math and science among the gifted.* Paper presented at the Annual Meeting of the American Educational Research Association. New Orleans, La.

Campbell, J. R., Connolly, C., & Pizzo, J. (1986a). *Self concept and attributions of gifted students in advanced high school science and math classes.* Paper presented at the Annual Meeting of the American Educational Research Association. San Francisco, CA.

Campbell, J. R., Connolly, C., & Pizzo, J. (1986b). *Self-concept and attributions of Westinghouse Talent Search Award recipients.* Paper presented at the Annual Meeting of the American Educational Research Association. San Franscisco, CA.

Connolly, C., & Primavera, L. (1983). *Characteristics of gifted students enrolled in Horizontal Enrichment Programs.* Paper presented at the 56th Annual Meeting of the National Association for Research in Science Teaching. Dallas, TX.

Dweck, S., Davidson, W., Nelson, S., & Enna, B. (1978). Sex differences in learned helplessness. *Developmental Psychology, 14,* 268-276.

Eccles, J. (1982). *Sex differences in achievement patterns.* Invited addess to the American Psychological Association. Washington, D.C.

Eccles, J. (1983). Expectancies, values, and academic behavior. In J. Spence (Ed.), *Achievement and achievement motivation.* San Francisco, CA: W.H. Freeman.

Eccles, J. (1984). *Do students turn off to math in junior high school?* Paper presented at the Annual Meeting of the American Educational Research Association. New Orleans, La.

Eccles, J., Adler, T., & Meece, J. L. (1984). Sex differences in achievement: A test of alternate theories. *Journal of Personality and Social Psychology, 46*(1), 26-43.

Fennema, E. (1982). *Women and mathematics: State of the art review.* Paper presented to the American Association for the Advancement of Science. Washington, D.C.

Fennema, E. (1983). *Final report: Research on relationship of spatial visualization and confidence to male/female mathematics achievement in grades 6-8.* Washington, D.C.: National Science Foundation.

Fennema, E. (1984). Girls, women, and mathematics. In E. Fennema, & M. J. Ayer (Eds.), *Women and education.* Berkeley, CA: McCutcheon.

Fennema, E., & Sherman, J. (1976). Fennema-Sherman Mathematics Attitude Scale: Instruments designed to measure attitudes toward the learning of mathematics by males and females. *Catalog of Selected Documents in Psychology, 6*(2), 31.

Fennema, E., & Sherman, J. (1977). Sex related differences in mathematics achievement, spatial visualization, and affective factors. *American Educational Research Journal,* 14(1), 51-71.

Fox, K., & Cohn, S. (1980). Sex differences in the development of precocious math talent. In L. Fox, L. Brody, & D. Tobin (Eds.), *Women and the mathematical mystique* (pp. 94-111). Baltimore, Md.: Johns Hopkins University Press.

Grant, L. (1983). *The socialization of white females in classrooms.* Paper presented at the Annual Meeting of the American Educational Research Association. Montreal, Canada.

Hilton, T. L., & Berglund, G. W. (1974). Sex differences in mathematical achievement: A longitudinal study. *Journal of Education Research, 67*(5), 231-237.

Hull, C. H., & Nie, N. H. (1981). *SPSS Update 7-9: New procedures and facilities for releases 7-9.* New York, NY: McGraw-Hill.

Lyons, L. (1980). *The relationship of parental modeling, parental reinforcement, academic and career interests to the enrollment of high school females in accelerated mathematics programs.* Paper presented at the Annual Meeting of the American Educational Research Association. Boston, Mass.

Marjoribanks, K. (1979). Family environments. In H. Walberg (Ed.), *Educational environments and effects.* Berkeley, CA: McCutcheon.

Meece, J. L. (1984). *Creating a supportive environment for young women in math and science.* Paper presented at the Annual Meeting of the American Educational Research Association. New Orleans, La.

Miller, S. D. (1984). *Differences in teacher-student interactions at the elementary and junior high school levels.* Paper presented at the Annual Meeting of the American Educational Research Association. New Orleans, La.

Peterson, P. L., & Fennema, E. (1983). *Effective teaching, student engagement in classroom activities and grade-related differences in learning mathematics.* Paper presented at the Wisconsin Center for Educational Research. Madison, Wisconsin.

Steinkamp, M. K., & Maehr, M. L. (1984). Gender differences in motivational orientations toward achievement in school science: A qualitative synthesis. *American Educational Research Journal. 21* (1), 39-59.

Stockard, J., & Wood, J. W. (1984). The myth of female underachievement: A re-examination of sex differences in academic underachievement. *American Educational Research Journal, 21* (4), 825-838.

Welch, M. (1983). *Characteristics and career choices of adolescent girls.* New York, NY: College Entrance Examination Board.

CHAPTER 7

THE INTERACTION OF TWO
ALPHABETS DURING READING

MARY TERESA RYAN
AND
EVELYN P. ALTENBERG*

Our study addresses the issue of whether a knowledge of
two alphabets has an effect on a bilingual individual's orthographic perception during reading. In particular, we will
examine the reading strategy of the Greek-English bilingual
in order to shed some light on the process of reading in general.

Psycholinguists have long been interested in bilingual
language processing. Much of the relevant literature suggests
that, while the bilingual can clearly function in one of his languages exclusively at will, it is difficult, if not impossible for
him to completely deactivate one of his languages while using
the other. It has been observed that the rules and structures
of one of his languages may interact with those of the other
language, even for the proficient bilingual. Evidence in support of bilingual language interaction comes from Sridhar and
Sridhar (1980), Blair and Harris (1981), and Altenberg and
Cairns (1983), who studied bilingual syntax, vocabulary, and
phonology, respectively. Further, it has been proposed that,
in order to keep his languages straight, the bilingual unconsciously uses some sort of comparison process, or 'language

*The authors would like to thank Helen Smith Cairns for her valu-
able comments and suggestions, and Harry J. Psomiades for his gener-
ous assistance in locating subjects for this study. A research assistant-
ship grant from Queens College, C.U.N.Y. to the first author provided
partial funding. The authors' names are listed in random order.

119

check mechanism,' to ensure that only the output of the contextually appropriate language processing system is used in
the final conceptual representation of input. This mechanism
is supported by Sridhar and Sridhar (1980) and Altenberg
and Cairns (1983).

Lukatela, Savic, Gligorijevic, Ognjenovic, and Turvey
(1978) have extended the language interaction inquiry into
the area of bialphabetic reading. Their subjects were speakers
of Serbo-Croatian, a language of Yugoslavia. Through an
interesting twist in the history of the development of the
Serbo-Croatian writing system, Serbo-Croatian is now written
in two different alphabets, the Roman and the Cyrillic. Native
speakers of this language are taught both alphabets in school
and become proficient at reading and writing in both. What
Lukatela and his colleagues questioned was whether speakers
of Serbo-Croatian are able to keep these two alphabets separate during reading. They found that their subjects could not
deactivate, or turn off, the Roman alphabet while reading
in Cyrillic, and vice versa. Clearly this supports an alphabetic
interaction model of reading for the bialphabetic speaker of
Serbo-Croatian.

Our study argues that further support for bilingual language interaction and alphabetic interaction can be found in
the reading strategy of the Greek-English bilingual: that is,
the adult who knows two different languages written with two
different alphabets.

Reading is a complicated process, and not all researchers
agree as to what steps and strategies are involved in deriving
meaning from the printed word. We will briefly describe three
current theories of reading: phonemic recoding, direct access,
and dual access.

The phonemic recoding theory proposes that each word
is stored in the lexicon ('mental dictionary') in a phonological
or sound-based code; a phonemic stage therefore mediates
initial visual perception and lexical assignment of grapheme
strings. In other words, in order to retrieve the meaning of
a printed word, the reader must first convert graphemes
("letters") into phonemes ("sounds") and then match this
sound sequence to the appropriate sound sequence stored in
the lexicon. This theory underlies the phonics method of reading instruction, where children are taught to pronounce each
letter in order to 'sound out' a word. The phonemic recoding
theory is supported by, for example, Corcoran (1967) and

Rubenstein, Lewis, and Rubenstein (1971), who found that nonwords which are pronounced like actual words (e.g., *brane*) are detected less readily than nonwords which do not sound like words (e.g., *melp*).

The direct access theory of reading postulates that the reader can go from the visual (graphemic) representation to the lexical representation of a word without accessing phonological information. The reader retrieves the meaning of a printed word based only on what the word looks like, not on what it sounds like. This theory underlies the 'look and say' or 'sight-reading' method of reading instruction, where children are taught to memorize words based on their visual properties alone. Baron (1973) is an example of evidence which supports the direct access theory. Baron asked subjects to indicate whether or not sentences were sensible. Some sentences contained homophones which sounded like words appropriate to the sentence (e.g., *Don't dew it.*) and some sentences contained homophones which did not sound like words appropriate to the sentence (e.g., *New I can't.*). He found no difference in responses to the two types of sentences.

According to the dual access theory, the reader uses a combination of direct access and phonemic recoding strategies. When the reader is confronted with a familiar visual configuration, he may employ a direct access strategy. That is, some letter strings occur so often that they may acquire an automatic, direct route from the letter pattern to the lexical representation. On the other hand, the reader may use a phonemic recoding strategy to decode unfamiliar words, relying on an unconscious use of grapheme to phoneme conversion rules to gain access to a lexical entry. Evidence from Davelaar, Coltheart, Besner, and Jonasson (1978), using a lexical decision task with homophones of various types, suggests that readers have two routes to lexical access, an orthographic one and a phonemic one, and that the activation of one route rather than the other is dependent upon its appropriateness to the requirements of the reading task at hand.

Evidence from speakers of English with dyslexia, as discussed by Coltheart (1984), also supports a dual access model of reading. One type of dyslexia involves an inability to read irregularly spelled words such as *colonel* but an ability to read nonwords such as **blik*. For individuals with this type of dyslexia, the direct access route is apparently impaired while the phonemic route is intact. Conversely, in another type of dyslexia, nonwords cannot be read while irregularly spelled words can, indicating that the phonemic route is impaired while the direct access route is intact. Apparently, the normal reader of English is able to use both of these routes for lexical access.

It is important to note that the type of orthography used to transcribe a language may influence the favoring of one strategy over another, as discussed by Hung and Tzeng (1981). Fang, Tzeng, and Alva (1981) propose that speakers of Chinese use a direct access strategy while reading their logographic or 'picture writing' script, which contains little sound information. On the other hand, strong evidence in support of the phoneme as the reading unit is found in studies of languages transcribed by phonologically shallow orthographies (Lukatela, Popadic, Ognjenovic, and Turvey, 1980; Feldman, 1981; Lukatela, Lorenc, Ognjenovic, and Turvey, 1981; Feldman and Turvey, 1983; Turvey, Feldman, and Lukatela, 1983; and others). A phonologically shallow orthography is one where the correspondence between letter and sound is regular and predictable. Greek, Italian, and Serbo-Croatian are examples of languages written with phonologically shallow orthographies. Thus, for example, an individual with no knowledge of Greek who was told what sound each Greek letter represents, could be shown a Greek word and, with little difficulty and a fair amount of accuracy, could figure out how to pronounce it.[1] A language whose orthography demonstrates such transparent grapheme to phoneme correspondences can be read efficiently with a phonemic recoding strategy.

This, however, is not the case for English, which is transcribed by a phonologically deep orthography. In such an orthography, the correspondence between letter and sound

[1]It must be noted that Greek orthography is not as phonetically precise as, for example, Serbo-Croatian orthography. Written Greek employs several diagraphs to represent sounds for which there are no individual letter symbols (e.g., the letter ν represents the phoneme /n/ and τ represents /t/, but ντ represents /d/). Other orthographic rules affect the pronounciation of certain consonants when they appear before vowel letters that represents + *high* sounds (e.g., γα represents /γα/, but γι represents /yi/). In addition, doubled consonant letters are pronounced as single consonants in most dialects. However, other than these orthographic rules, which are few in number and operate in a regular and predictable fashion, Greek orthography is regular and transparent and exhibits the major characteristics of a phonologically shallow orthography.

is opaque and the spelling is adapted to include morphological information as well as phonological information. One does not always know how to pronounce an English word on the basis of its spelling. For example, the word *sign* and the first four letters of the word *signature* are not pronounced the same, yet by the way these words look we can tell that they are related. The fact that many English words provide such visual clues as well as sound clues in their spelling perhaps best explains why the speaker of English may use a dual access strategy while reading. We shall argue that Greek-English bilinguals use a phonemic recoding strategy in the English proofreading experiment described below.

A proofreading task was constructed in which reading passages were transformed to include errors that were phonological in nature. In particular, the experiment was designed to take advantage of inter-alphabetic ambiguous letters in Greek and English. These ambiguous letters are similar in appearance in both the English and Greek alphabets but represent different sounds in each language. An example of an ambiguous letter is *p*, which represents the phoneme /p/ in English but the phoneme /r/ in Greek.

Greek-English bilingual and English monolingual subjects were asked to proofread English passages for 'typing' errors, with instructions to circle the incorrect letter in the word. There were three types of stimuli: a) English Random typos, created by substituting an English letter that is not ambiguous for another English letter, e.g., *g* substituted for *w* in the word *without*, creating the typo **githout*; b) Greek Random typos, created by substituting an ambiguous letter for an unrelated English letter, e.g., *p* substituted for *f* in the word *first*, creating the typo **pirst*; and c) Greek Phonemic typos, created by substituting an ambiguous letter for the phonologically related English letter, e.g., substituting *p* for *r* in the word *floor*, creating the typo **floop*, where *p* represents phonemic /r/ in Greek.

If Greek-English bilinguals completely deactivate the Greek alphabet when reading English, then the detection pattern for all three types of stimuli should be the same for both the bilingual subjects and the monolingual subjects. If Greek-English bilinguals are affected in a general way by the presence of inter-alphabetic ambiguous letters, simply by being more alert to them and therefore more careful when reading them, then the bilinguals should have a higher detection rate for Greek Random and Greek Phonemic stimuli than for English Random stimuli. Finally, if the bilingual reader recodes letters phonemically, and does so for both Greek and English phoneme-to-grapheme correspondences, then there are two possibilities. If the bilingual, upon seeing *floop, converts the letter p to both the phonemes /p/ and /r/, he may be less skilled at detecting the *floop error since it could be read as floo/r/. Under this scenario, Greek Phonemic errors will be detected less readily than other errors. On the other hand, if the bilingual converts the letter p to both /p/ and /r/, but then uses a 'language check mechanism' to see if the language-appropriate conversion rules are being used, he will realize that using p to represent the sound /r/ is not appropriate for English (although it is for Greek). The earlier conversion to /r/, however, will have helped alert the bilingual to what the correct English word should be and hence to the identification of p as the typo. Under this scenario, the bilingual will be better at detecting ambiguous phonological typos (Greek Phonemic) than the other two kinds of typos.

Thus, if the bilingual subjects are affected in some way by their knowledge of the Greek alphabet, their overall pattern of responses to the three types of stimuli will be different from that of the monolinguals. If the bilinguals recode phonemically in the Greek alphabet, even in an English reading task, then the detection rate for Greek Phonemic typos will be different from the detection rate for the other two types of stimuli.

METHOD

Materials

Six proofreading passages of approximately 350 words each were constructed. The passages were taken from a high intermediate ESL text (Byrne, 1974) and altered to include letter substitutions. Each passage was followed by a comprehension question to ensure that low error detection rates were not due to poor comprehension of the text and to ensure reading for content as well as for typos.

For the Greek letter substitutions, we selected three lower case letters that have a similar appearance in each alphabet but represent different sounds: p represents /r/ in Greek, v represents /n/ in Greek, and n represents /i/ in Greek. In the Greek phonemic condition, these were substituted for the phonologically related English letter, e.g. *floor—*floop*. In the Greek Random condition, these letters replaced letters unrelated to Greek orthography, e.g., *first—>*pirst*.[2]

Three English letters that are not ambiguous were chosen for the English random condition: *g, m,* and *s.* These were selected because they correspond to *p, v,* and *n* with respect to the presence of ascending or descending features (McConkie and Rayner, 1975), average frequency of occurrence per thousand letters in English (Pratt, 1939), and relative frequency of occurrence (Wolfe, 1970).

Half of the substitutions for each letter were made in word initial and half in word final position, as it has been shown that the position of a letter within a word plays a role in the ease with which it can be detected (e.g., Drewnowski and Healy, 1980). Each passage contained six Greek Random substitutions and six Greek Phonemic substitutions evenly divided among *p, v,* and *n* and with one word initial and one word final substitution per letter. These were matched by 12 English random substitutions, with two word initial and two word final substitutions for each of *g, m,* and *s.*

Substitutions were constrained such that there were no substitutions for words of less than three or more than eleven letters in length. Substitutions for very low frequency letters were avoided. None of the errors were placed in function words, tense morphemes, or *-ing* or *ent* (*-ant*) suffixes (Drewnowski and Healy, 1982). We attempted to vary the occurrence of each type of substitution so that it appeared in both common and uncommon words (Healy, 1980) in approximately equal distribution throughout the texts. However, since the passages were taken from an ESL text, the vocabulary did not include any truly unusual or uncommon words. Attempts were also made, as much as possible, to control for the location of errors with respect to the semantic focus of the sentence (Cutler and Fodor, 1979). The number and types of substitutions were distributed fairly evenly throughout the texts.

Letter combinations that are visually as well as phonologically acceptable in English were used whenever possible, with the exception of the ambiguous letter substitution *n.* This was impossible to place in a visually acceptable context due to the fact that it represents the vowel /i/ in Greek. There are also

[2]No ambiguous letter substitutions were placed such that the resulting letter string contained a possible Greek digraph.

very few common English words with word initial /i/, so these had to be interpolated into the texts. It was necessary to repeat two of these words in two separate texts (*even* and *equal/equally*) ; care was taken to ensure that these repeated words did not occur in consecutive texts.

Normal pica type was used for the texts. *p, v,* and *n* were not altered to appear as they would in a Greek text, since they are sufficiently similar in the two alphabets to be taken as equivalent. (Interletter similarity is a factor in letter confusability; Holbrook, 1978.) Further, normal English type was used because that is what subjects are accustomed to reading in English.

Subjects

There were 23 Greek-English bilinguals and 23 English monolingual subjects. All were undergraduate students at Queens College between the ages of 19 and 33. Each subject completed a language background questionnaire.

The monolingual subjects did not consider themselves to be bilingual in any languages. None had ever studied Greek or been exposed to Greek in their homes. The bilingual subjects were all native speakers of Greek. Nine of the bilinguals had begun learning English at or before the age of 12, and 14 after the age of 12. The bilinguals' questionnaire included a scale for self-rating of comparable overall proficiency in Greek and English. Subjects' average rating was 1.65, where 1 = much better in Greek, 4 = equally skilled in Greek and English, and 7 = much better in English. Thus, on the whole, bilingual subjects were dominant in Greek.

Procedure

All subjects were given the following instructions : "You will be given a series of passages. Each passage contains a number of typing mistakes. When you find a mistake, your job is to circle the letter that is incorrect. A word will not have more than one mistake in it." An example followed, and the instructions continued: "After you correct the mistakes in each passage, you will be asked a question about the passage you have been reading. Do not turn the page until you are instructed to do so. You will have two minutes for each passage."

RESULTS

Table 1 indicates the percentage of correct identification of typos for monolingual and bilingual subjects under each of the three conditions. Since some of the bilingual subjects were unable to finish each passage, the data from the last one third of each passage was omitted from this analysis for all subjects. This allows us to be confident that the percentage reflects typo detection rather than passage completion. Further, any subject who responded incorrectly on more than three of the comprehension questions was omitted.

TABLE 1
SCORES ANALYZED BY STIMULUS CONDITION

	English Random e.g., *github (without)	Greek Random e.g., *pirst (first)	Greek Phonemic e.g., *floop (floor)	M
Monolinguals	94.74	96.60	97.44	96.26
Bilinguals	78.84	80.80	89.16	82.93

Note. Scores indicate percentage of correct detection of typos.

A repeated measures analysis of variance was done, with one within factor (stimulus: type of letter substitution) and one between factor (subject group: monolingual vs. bilingual). The analysis reveals a significant effect of type of letter substitution, over all subjects: $(F(2,88) = 22.44, p < .001$. There was also a significant effect of subject group: $F(1,44) = 27.38, p < .001$. Of particular significance was the finding that there was an interaction of type of substitution with subject group: $F(2,88) = 9.57, p < .001$. That is, bilinguals did not have the same pattern of responses to the three types of letter substitutions as did the monolinguals.

Comparisons of means for individual types of letter substitutions were made using a Tukey range test, at the .05 level of significance. According to the Tukey range test, there was no significant difference in error detection for monolinguals among the three types of stimuli. That is, 94.74 = 96.60 = 97.44. For the bilingual subjects, there was no significant difference in error detection between the English Random and Greek Random conditions (78.84 = 80.80). Of greatest interest here is the finding that, for the bilinguals, the percentage of error detection in the Greek Phonemic condition was higher than in the other two conditions (89.16 > 78.84; 89.16 > 80.80).

Table 2 indicates the results in terms of letter position, word initial vs. word final. Overall, there was no effect of

TABLE 2

WORD INITIAL VS. WORD FINAL SCORES

| | English Random e.g., *githout (without) | | Greek Random e.g., *pirst (first) | | Greek Phonemic e.g., *floop (floor) | | M |
	Word Initial	Word Final	Word Initial	Word Final	Word Initial	Word Final	
Monoliguals	97.10	92.39	98.55	94.65	97.99	96.89	96.26
Bilinguals	80.52	77.17	78.99	82.61	87.63	90.68	82.93
M	88.81	84.78	88.77	88.63	92.81	93.79	89.60

Note. Scores indicate percentage of correct detection of typos.

letter position: $F(1,44) = 1.27$, $p > .05$, although there was a significant interaction of letter position and subject group: $F(1,44) = 5.33$, $p < .05$. The interaction of type of stimulus with initial vs. final position approached significance: $F(2,88) = 2.85$, $p = .063$. The interaction of type of stimulus, initial vs. final position and subject group was not significant: $F(2,88) < 1$.

Table 3 indicates the percentage of correct error detections analyzed by individual letter. A repeated measures analysis of variance was done on the Greek Random and Greek Phonemic letters. (The analysis could not include the English Random letters since these are different graphemes, and could not statistically be collapsed with the Greek ambiguous letters to provide an overall effect of individual letter.)

There was no overall effect of individual letters, although the effect approaches significance: $F(2,88) = 2.81$, $p = .066$. There was no significant letter by subject group interaction:

TABLE 3
SCORES ANALYZED BY INDIVIDUAL LETTER

	n	*v*	*p*
All Subjects	89.67	91.94	92.19
Monolinguals	96.96	96.74	97.79
Bilinguals	82.39	87.14	86.59
Initial Position	90.87	90.13	92.21
Final Position	88.48	93.75	92.17
Greek Random	85.87	89.68	91.67
Greek Phonemic	93.48	94.20	92.72
Monolinguals, Greek Random	96.52	95.11	98.19
Bilinguals, Greek Random	75.22	84.24	85.15
Monolinguals, Greek Phonemic	97.39	98.37	97.39
Bilinguals, Greek Phonemic	89.57	90.04	88.04

Note. Scores indicate percentage of correct detection of typos. While stimulus letters appear here in italics, on the actual task they appeared in normal pica letters and were no different in appearance from the other letters in the task passages.

$F(2,88) = 2.35$, $p > .05$. That is, monolinguals and bilinguals did not respond differently to individual letters. The interaction between type of stimulus and letter was significant over all subjects: $F(2,88) = 3.23$, $p < .05$, as was the interaction between letter and initial vs. final position: $F(2,88) = 3.44$, $p < .05$. There was a significant interaction of type of stimulus, initial vs. final position, letter and subject group: $F(2,88) = 3.35$, $p < .05$, and a significant interaction of initial vs. final position, letter, and subject group: $F(2,88) = 8.44$, $p < .001$. The interaction of type of stimulus, letter, and subject group approached significance: $F(2,88) = 2.71$, $p = .072$, as did the interaction of type of stimulus, initial vs. final position, and letter: $F(2,88) = 2.76$, $p = .069$.

DISCUSSION

Among the major findings of the experiment are, first,

that there was a significant difference, overall, between monolingual and bilingual subjects. The monolinguals were better
at detecting errors than the bilingual subjects. This is pre-
sumably due to the fact that the bilingual subjects were less
proficient in English than in Greek, and less proficient than
the English monolingual subjects. This conclusion is supported
by the fact that the average number of incorrect responses to
the comprehension questions was .48 for the monolingual sub-
pects and 1.17 for the bilingual subjects.

The results also indicate a significant stimulus by group
interaction. That is, the bilingual subjects did not have the
same pattern of error detection for the three types of stimuli
as did the monolingual subjects. The difference in patterning
reveals that the bilingual subjects' knowledge of two alphabets
played a role in their ability to detect the various kinds of
typos, a finding which supports an alphabetic interaction model
of reading.

We can pin this interaction down more precisely when
scores for the individual types of stimuli are examined in
greater detail. Monolingual subjects scored equally well on
all three types of test items while bilingual subjects scored
as well on English Random as on Greek Random stimuli, but
scored best on Greek Phonemic items. This finding supports
the phonemic recoding hypothesis for these individuals, since
only phonemic recoding can account for the advantage of Greek
Phonemic over Greek Random stimuli. More specifically, the
results support a model in which graphemes are converted to
phonemes, with bilingual, bialphabetic individuals converting
ambiguous graphemes into two different phonemes. The bilingual then uses a language check mechanism to ensure that
the contextually appropriate grapheme to phoneme conversion
rules have been used. In this task, the language check mechanism revealed that, e.g., $p \longrightarrow /r/$ is not appropriate for English, and hence that *floop could not be read as floor. Thus,
the language check caused the bilingual to detect the typo,
while phonemic recoding into Greek aided the bilingual in
determining what the incorrect word should have been. This
strategy was not a conscious one, since post-test questioning
of the bilingual subjects revealed that they had had no idea
as to what the experiment was about; in particular, they had
not noticed the presence of the ambiguous letters. Thus, the
model of bialphabetic reading which we outline here is an
automatic, unconscious one.

While there was no effect of individual Greek letters on overall error detection rates, the interaction statistics reveal that bilingual subjects were less able to detect n in the Greek Random than in the Greek Phonemic condition. This finding is what one would expect, given the lower detection rates for the Greek Random vs. the Greek Phonemic condition. However, the fact that the detection rate for bilingual subjects in the Greek Random condition was considerably lower for n than for v and p (75.22 vs. 84.24 and 85.15) remains a puzzling finding.

It is important to recognize that at least two factors were steering bilingual subjects toward the use of a phonemic recoding strategy. One was the nature of the proofreading task itself, since it requires subjects to identify incorrect letters. The second was the dominance of Greek over English for the bilingual subjects. As noted above, Greek has a shallow orthography, which would lead individuals to favor a phonemic recoding approach when reading in Greek. The bilingual subjects may have transferred this strategy to reading in English during the process of acquiring English. Thus, one may find more evidence of phonemic recoding in an English task with speakers whose dominant language has a shallow orthography, such as Greek, than with speakers whose dominant language has a deep orthography, such as French. This transfer of reading strategy needs to be studied by both the psycholinguist and the educator, for, as we have seen, the Greek speaker acquiring English needs to learn not only a new language and a new alphabet, but a new orthographic system that is suited to a direct access reading strategy as well as to the phonemic recoding strategy which he has been using for his native language. (It should be noted that the term *transfer* is being used here to refer to the transfer of a reading strategy, not to the transfer of grapheme to phoneme conversion rules. The results for the bilingual subjects reveal that they were well aware that in English, e.g., p converts to /p/ and not to /r/.)

In summary, our results support a phonemic recoding, interaction model of bialphabetic reading: Greek-English bilingual subjects unconsciously used their knowledge of both alphabets to convert graphemes to both English and Greek phonemes in this English proofreading task.

REFERENCES

Altenberg, E. P., & Cairns, H. S. (1983). The effects of phonotactic constraints on lexical processing in bilingual and monolingual subjects. *Journal of Verbal Learning and Verbal Behavior, 22,* 174-188.

Baron, J. Phonemic stage not necessary for reading. (1973). *Quarterly Journal of Experimental Psychology, 25,* 241-246.

Blair, D., & Harris, R. J. (1981). A test of interlingual interaction in comprehension by bilinguals. *Journal of Psycholinguistic Research,* 10, 457-467.

Byrne, D. (1974). *Intermediate Comprehension Passages.* Rowley, Massachusetts: Longman-Newbury House.

Coltheart, M. (1984). Writing systems and reading disorders. In L. Henderson (Ed.) *Orthographies and Reading.* Hillsdale, New Jersey: Lawrence Erlbaum Associates.

Corcoran, D. W. (1967). Acoustic factors in proofreading. *Nature, 214,* 851.

Cutler, A., & Fodor, J. A. (1979). Semantic focus and sentence comprehension. *Cognition, 7* (1), 49-59.

Davelaar, E., Coltheart, M., Besner, D. & Jonasson, J. T. (1978). Phonological recoding and lexical access. *Memory and Cognition, 6* (4), 391-402.

Drewnowski, A., & Healy, A. F. (1980). Missing *-ing* in reading: letter detection errors on word endings. *Journal of Verbal Learning and Verbal Behavior, 19,* 247-262.

Drewnowski, A., & Healy, A. F. (1982). Phonetic factors in letter detection: a reevaluation. *Haskins Laboratories: Status Report on Speech Research, SR-70,* 77-98.

Fang, S. P., Tzeng, O. J. L., & Alva, L. (1981). Intralanguage vs. interlanguage Stroop effects in two types of writing systems. *Memory and Cognition, 9* (6), 609-617.

Feldman, L. B. (1981). Visual word recognition in Serbo-Croatian is necessarily phonological. *Haskins Laboratories: Status Report on Speech Research, SR-66,* 167-200.

Feldman, L. B., & Turvey, M. T. (1983). Word recognition in Serbo-Croatian is phonologically analytic. *Journal of Experimental Psychology: Human Perception and Performance, 9,* 288-298.

Healy, A. F. (1980). Proofreading errors on the word *the*: New evidence on reading units. *Journal of Experimental Psychology: Human Perception and Performance, 6,* 45-57.

Holbrook, M. B. (1978). Effect of subjective interletter similarity, perceived word similarity, and contextual variables on the recognition of letter substitutions in a proofreading task. *Perceptual and Motor Skills, 47,* 251-258.

Hung, D. L., & Tzeng, O. J. L. (1981). Orthographic variations and visual information processing. *Haskins Laboratories: Status Report on Speech Research, SR-66,* 119-166.

Lukatela, G., Lorenc, B., Ognjenovic, P., & Turvey, M. T. (1981). A word superiority effect in a phonetically precise orthography. *Language and Speech, 24* (2), 173-183.

Lukatela, G., Popadic, D., Ognjenovic, P., & Turvey, M. T. (1980). Lexical decision in a phonologically shallow orthography. *Memory and Cognition, 8* (2), 124-132.

Lukatela, G., Savic, M., Gligorijevic, B., Ognjenovic, P., & Turvey, M. T. (1978). Bi-alphabetic lexical decision. *Language and Speech, 21* (2), 142-165.

McConkie, G. W., & Rayner, K. (1975). The span of the effective stimulus during a fixation in reading. *Perception and Psychophysics, 17,* 578-586.

Pratt, F. (1939). *Secret and Urgent: The Story of Codes and Ciphers.* Indianapolis.

Rubenstein, H., Lewis, S. S., & Rubenstein, M. A. (1971). Evidence for phonemic recoding in visual word recognition. *Journal of Verbal Learning and Verbal Behavior, 10,* 645-657.

Sridhar, S.N., & Sridhar, K. K. (1980). The syntax and psycholinguistics of bilingual code mixing. *Canadian Journal of Psychology, 34,* 407-416.

Turvey, M. T., Feldman, L. B., & Lukatela, G. (1984). The Serbo-Croatian orthography constrains the reader to a phonologically analytic strategy. In L. Henderson (Ed.), *Orthographies and Reading.* Hillsdale, New Jersey: Lawrence Erlbaum Associates.

Wolfe, J. R. (1970). *Secret Writing: The Craft of the Cryptographer.* New York: McGraw-Hill Book Company.

CHAPTER 8

COGNITIVE STYLE AND THE READING PROCESS IN GREEK-ENGLISH BILINGUALS

TERRY TCHACONAS

Readers are active participants in the reading act–their thought language cue not only their expected responses (printed words), but also their observed responses (deviations from printed words). This consideration leads one to conclude that readers' miscues, or deviations from print are not random. They use the interrelated cue system of language (graphophonic, syntactic and semantic) in conjunction with their background knowledge to construct meaning from print. The ways in which readers employ these cue systems when reading orally may be referred to as their oral reading strategies.

Several studies have appeared in the literature that discuss the cognitive styles (modes of attending, perceiving, remembering and thinking) of bilinguals indicate how cognitive style may affect their ability to learn to read in English (Hodes, 1976; Barrera, 1978; DeSilva, 1978; Eaton, 1979; Spiridakis, 1982).

Field-dependence/independence is one dimension of cognitive style orientation that may influence how the reader processes print and derives meaning from it. Witkin, Moore, Goodenough, and Cox (1962) have employed the terms field-dependence and field-independence to explain the extent to

This research is based on portions of the author's doctoral dissertation submitted to Teachers College, Columbia University.

which a person perceives analytically and overcomes an embedding context. Field-dependence refers to the mode of perception at one extreme of the performance range where the prevailing field strongly dominates perception (global). Such an individual would tend to perceive a word in its entirety while reading. At the opposite end of the performance range lies the mode of perception referred to as field-independence where items are experienced as more or less separate from the surrounding field (analytical). In principle, this individual would tend to be more successful than his field-dependent counterpart in being able to break down an unknown word into its phonetic parts while reading.

When individuals approach a reading task, they are confronted with a situation of response uncertainty (Smith, 1978). As a means of reducing this uncertainty, the readers impose their own organization upon the task. They select only what they need from the cueing systems in order to construct meaning from print. Their selection is probably influenced by their own established patterns of coping with environmental stimuli. Cognitive style orientation, in particular field-dependence/field-independence, may very well influence the types of cues that readers select in order to construct meaning and to impose organization onto the reading task, as well as the extent to which they use those particular cues. It was patterns of these cue selection strategies (as identified through miscue analysis) in relation to a particular cognitive style orientation (field-dependence/field-independence) that this research focused upon in order to better understand this particular sample of Greek bilingual children's oral reading.

To achieve the purpose of the descriptive study, these questions were asked:

1. What differences exist, if any, in the oral reading strategies used by the subjects while reading in English compared to their oral reading strategies while reading in Greek?

2. What differences exist, if any, in the oral reading strategies for field-dependent (FD) Greek bilingual children as opposed to field-independent (FI) Greek bilingual children while reading in both English and Greek.

METHOD

Sample

The students who participated in this study attended a New York City public elementary school which has approximately a 25% Greek population. Twelve second grade students were chosen from a group of children who had been in a Greek bilingual program since kindergarten. The Language Dominance/Language Proficiency test (LD/LP) was administered to each child to ensure that each student was sufficiently proficient in both English and Greek. The LD/LP test developed by Michopoulos (1980), was used in this study because it is the only instrument of its kind for Greek-American students with established validity and reliability data (Mylonas, 1981). According to the LD/LP test, students are considered "sufficiently proficient" in English and Greek if they score within one standard deviation of the mean or higher. This was an important condition for selection because each subject had to be able to read textual materials in both English and Greek.

All the children in the school's Greek bilingual program had been receiving instruction in their native language (Greek) as well as in English from kindergarten. Since children progress at varied rates, and because the primary purpose of this study was to investigate the ways in which cognitive style might affect the extent of use of different reading strategies by oral readers as they construct meaning from print, a specified grade level of reading was not a condition for selection of subjects. Of course, each child took standardized silent reading tests in English as part of the school's regular testing program and these were examined for possible linkages with the miscue analysis results. The standardized reading test that these particular subjects took was the California Achievement Test (CAT)—Level 12, Form C.

This particular sample of bilingual children were in a transitional bilingual program which meant that their Greek instruction was diminishing as their English language skills improved. For example, when the subjects entered kindergarten they received approximately an equal number of hours of reading readiness in both English and Greek. When reading was formally introduced in the first grade through primarily a phonics oriented system of beginning reading, the children were taught to read simultaneously in two languages (approx-

imately 30% of total instructional time was devoted to reading in each language). Toward the end of the children's second
grade school year (April), when this study began, the instructional time devoted to Greek reading was decreasing (approximately 15% of the total instructional time or about 90
hours per year) while the time devoted to English reading
instruction was increasing (approximately 45% of the total
instructional time or about 270 hours per year).

In addition to the CAT, a child in second grade Greek
bilingual program took the Children's Embedded Figures Test
(CEFT) developed by Witkin, et al (1971) and after a
median split was performed on the scores (they can range
from 0 to 25), six "proficient" subjects with scores (14, 15,
16) that extended most extremely beyond one standard deviation of the mean were considered field-independent (FI) for
the purposes of this study, and six "proficient" subjects whose
scores (5, 7, 8) extended most extremely beyond a negative
one standard deviation from the mean were considered field-
dependent (FD). To safeguard the study against any research
bias or influence in observation, the FI and FD children were
not known.

Procedure

All subjects were asked to read orally one entire unfamiliar story from their English basal reading text and another
unfamiliar story from their Greek basal reading text, with the
selection being of sufficient length and difficulty to generate a
minimum number of 25 miscues (see Goodman & Burke, 1972).
Upon completing each tape-recorded selection, the readers
were asked to retell orally everything about the story that
they could remember. Next, probe questions were asked based
on the information supplied by the students in order to aid
them in remembering what they had comprehended but perhaps forgotten to retell. This retelling was also recorded as
well as assessed and a retelling score was determined.

The oral reading miscues generated in both languages
by the subjects were coded and analyzed according to procedures detailed by Goodman & Burke (1972), described and
compared in order to: (1) compile a comparison profile of
the English and Greek oral reading strategies and behavior
of each subject; and (2) compile a comparison profile of the

English and Greek oral reading strategies and behavior of each group of subjects identified as FD and FI.

The task of analyzing the data began after all the audio-taping of the readings by the subjects had been completed. The tapes of the oral readings were listened to as many times as necessary to ensure that all deviations from the text were precisely identified. The second step involved the coding of these deviations or miscues. The Reading Miscue Inventory-RMI (Goodman & Burke, 1972) was used for providing general guidelines in determining the inclusion or exclusion of miscues. Included in the count were: (1) insertions, omissions, substitutions and reversals of a prefix, suffix, or word regardless of whether they were subsequently corrected; (2) only the first complete word or nonword substitution when a reader makes repeated attempts on a word; and (3) complex miscues involving more than a one-for-one substitution, insertion, omission, or reversal.

The adapted version of the RMI used in this study enabled classification of the miscues as follows:

1. Graphic similarity. How much does the miscue look like that which was expected?

2. Sound similarity. How much does the miscue sound like that which was expected?

3. Grammatical function. Is the grammatical function of the miscue the same as the grammatical function of the word in the text?

4. Correction. Is the miscue corrected?

5. Grammatical acceptability. Does the miscue occur in a structure which is grammatically acceptable?

6. Semantic acceptability. Does the miscue occur in a structure which is semantically acceptable?

7. Does the miscue result in a change of meaning?

To give the reader a better idea of how the miscues were coded, another excerpt from one of the subject's English reading is provided and an explanation as to how the miscue was coded in each of the RMI categories:

sky
Soon the sly fox knocked on the door of another house.

1. Graphic Similarity. Since the miscue or observed response (sky) has 66.7% (2 out of 3) of the same letters as the expected response (sly), it is coded as having high graphic similarity (above 50% graphic and sound similarity needed between the miscue and the expected response for a high graphic and sound similarity coding).

2. Sound Similarity. Since the miscue or observed response (sly) has only 50% (1 out of 2) of the same sounds as the expected response (the consonant clusters sk and sl are each considered one phoneme), it is coded as having partial sound similarity with the expected response.

3. Grammatical Function. Since the grammatical function of the miscue (sky is a noun) is different from the grammatical function of the expected response (sly is an adjective), it is coded as having a difference in a grammatical function from the expected response. If it is impossible to determine a miscue's grammatical function, an indeterminate coding is assigned.

4. Correction. The miscue was not corrected as indicated by the absence of a c next to the miscue.

5. Grammatical Acceptability. The miscue is grammatically acceptable only with the sentence portion that comes before it and thus is coded as having partial grammatical acceptability.

6. Semantic Acceptability. The miscue is semantically acceptable only with the sentence portion that comes before it and thus is coded as having partial semantic acceptability.

7. Meaning Change. Since the uncorrected miscue changes the meaning of the sentence, it is coded as causing an extensive change in meaning.

In addition, the number of miscues per hundred words (MPHW) was compiled for each reading in each language. It was hoped that this statistic would be indicative of the relative difficulty of the selections in the two languages.

After classifying each of the subjects, miscues in the

above categories, descriptive statistics were obtained in each language for individuals and groups, identified by cognitive style orientation, consisting of percentages, frequencies and means. Comprehension proficiency was determined according to patterns of responses obtained for the categories of correction, semantic acceptability and meaning change. Grammatical relationships were determined according to the patterns of responses obtained for the categories of correction, grammatical acceptability and semantic acceptability.

The statistical analysis included a retelling score which measured the reader's understanding of that which already has been read. According to the RMI, this score is obtained by adding points designated to show the reader's awareness of character analysis, content or events, and extra information such as theme, plot as well as personal reaction.

A comparative profile for each subject was compiled which summarized all statistical findings in each language. Group comparisons in each of the categories of the RMI was depicted in terms of tables and frequency distributions. It was hoped that at this point, patterns would emerge that would not only show particular reading strategies used by field-independents as opposed to field-dependents but also whether the subjects were demonstrating the same reading behavior in reading both languages or whether the reading strategies employed by these bilinguals varied according to the language being read.

RESULTS

The English and Greek oral reading strategies (using the RMI) of six subjects designated by the CEFT as field-dependent (FD) and another six subjects designated as field-independent (FI) were explored and the results compared to determine if differences exist between groups and between languages read and whether patterns of oral reading strategies can be described.

The summary of the results in Table 1 reveal that the subjects identified as FI and FD tended to look consistently distinct across the two languages. That is, the majority of the analyzed categories for both the Greek and English reading tasks did indicate patterns that might possibly be linked to one's characteristic degree of field-dependency-independency.

TABLE 1
SUMMARY OF THE RESULTS

Category of Reading Miscue Inventory (RMI)	English		Analysis	Greek		Analysis
	FD	FI		FD	FI	
Graphic Similarity	87.5	90.5	No difference between groups.	98	96	No difference between groups—parallels English. Both groups paid much No difference between groups—parallels English.
Sound Similarity (High and Partial)	82.4	85.3	No difference between groups.	95.7	94	Both groups cued on sound similarities to a greater extent in Greek than in English.
Grammatical Function (Identical and Indeterminate)	61.7	68.6	FIs produced more miscues whose grammatical function conformed to those of the expected responses than did FDs.	79.3	89.5	FIs produced more miscues whose grammatical function conformed to those of the expected responses—parallels English. Both groups produced considerably more miscues in Greek that conformed to those of the expected responses than in English.

Note. The values represent percentages.

Grammatical Acceptability (Total)	50	55.3	FIs were more grammatically aware than FDs.	59.3	61.3	No difference between groups—does not parallel English. Both groups were more grammatically aware in Greek than in English.
Semantic Acceptability (Total and Partial)	56.7	66	FIs cued more on the semantic system than did FDs.	47.4	50	No difference between groups—result does not parallel English. Both groups were considerably more aware of semantic cues in English than in Greek.
Grammatical Relationships (Strength and Partial)	64.7	70	FIs were more aware of grammatical relationships than FDs.	65.3	71.4	FIs were more aware of grammatical relationships than FDs—parallels English. No difference between language read for both groups.
Meaning Change (Minimum and No Change)	32	38.7	FIs generated more miscues which resulted in little or no meaning change than did FDs.	30.7	42	FIs generated more miscues which resulted in little or no meaning change than did FDs—parallels English. No difference between languages read for both groups.

TABLE 1 (continued)
SUMMARY OF THE RESULTS

Category of Reading Miscue Inventory (RMI)	English		Analysis	Greek		Analysis
	FD	FI		FD	FI	
Correction	28	28.7	No difference between groups.	13.3	15.6	No difference between groups–parallels English. Both groups corrected far more in English, indicating a greater attention to meaning in English than in Greek reading.
Correction Strategies and Grammatical Acceptability (Total and Partial not corrected)	91.25	82	FIs were grammatically more aware as they left uncorrected a greater percentage of total and partial grammatically acceptable miscues than did FDs.	83.2	83.4	Not enough data generated in this category to warrant analysis of results.
Correction Strategies and Grammatical Aceptability (Not acceptable corrected)	17.5	22.5	FIs more grammatically aware than FDs as they more frequently corrected grammatically unacceptable miscues.	21.4	23.7	Not enough data generated in this category to warrant analysis of results.

Category					
Correction Strategies and Semantic Acceptability (Total and Partial not corrected)	60.3	67.5	FIs were semantically more aware as they left uncorrected a greater percentage of total and partial grammatically acceptable miscues than did FDs.	43.7	45.9	Not enough data generated in this category to warrant analysis of results.
Correction Strategies and Semantic Acceptability (Totally acceptable corrected)	16	15.3	No difference between groups.	13.3	12.8	Not enough data generated in this category to warrant analysis of results.
Comprehending (No Loss and Partial Loss)	52	62	FIs comprehended more during the reading act than did FDs.	38.7	52	FIs comprehended more during the reading act than did FDs—parallels English. Both groups comprehend more while reading in English.
Retelling	52.5	78	FIs retold a greater amount of their reading than did FDs.	50	58.3	FIs retold a greater amount of their reading than did the FDs—parallels English. Both groups were able to relate a greater amount of their reading in English than of their reading in Greek.

For 8 of the 10 categories for which sufficient data were generated to warrant analysis, the Greek reading behavior of the FI and FD subjects paralleled their behavior while reading in English. Overall, it can be said that both groups reading in both languages attended to visual and auditory details to a great extent but the fewer miscues generated by the FIs indicates that they attended more carefully to the parts whereas the FDs were more apt to miscue by looking at the whole rather than its components. Furthermore, the FI subjects appeared to bring more meaning and understanding of language to the texts than did the FDs. Two categories, grammatical acceptability and semantic acceptability of miscues, failed to reflect such parallelism in both languages even though the FIs' miscues were more acceptable in English and Greek (the 2% difference, however, between groups in the Greek reading for these categories was not enough for meaningful comparison). For the categories relating correction strategies to grammatical and semantic acceptability of miscues, not enough data were generated for meaningful analysis.

However, the pattern of FD and FI readers using oral reading strategies in a distinct way across languages does not mean that the nature of the reading was the same for both languages. All subjects made more miscues while reading in Greek (16.4 miscue per hundred words rate compared to 7.7 in the English reading) and tended to depend more on graphophonic and grammatical cues while reading in Greek, (perhaps due to the more phonetic nature of Greek) whereas the subjects tended to be more aware of semantic cues while reading in English as reflected by the higher comprehending and retelling scores in English.

Overall, the subjects in both languages displayed to a greater or lesser extent the general reading strategies of sampling, predicting, testing, confirming, and correcting, where necessary in conjunction with the use of the graphophonic, semantic and grammatical cues as well as their prior knowledge in order to get meaning from print. That there is one reading process that manifests itself across readers and across languages seems probable but within that process there is so much variation, especially among younger readers, that individual modes of processing and type of language being read should be taken into account.

GENERAL CONCLUSIONS AND IMPLICATIONS

There seem to be general tentative conclusions generated from the findings that can be drawn from the analysis of the reading behavior of the bilingual second-grade subjects who participated in this study, and these conclusions provide certain implications for instructional programs, as noted below:

1. *Common Oral Reading Strategies.*

The utilization of oral reading strategies (i.e., sampling, predicting, testing, confirming, correcting when necessary in conjunction with the graphophonic, semantic, and syntactic cueing systems) was in evidence for both languages read in this study but the extent to which they were used by the subjects varied. In other words, the differences were more a matter of degree rather than of kind. The data support previous research findings which also indicate that there is one reading process which has been mastered to a lesser extent (the subjects' reading in Greek), or to a greater extent (the subjects' reading in English). This conclusion argues for common methodologies across languages while teaching reading. Reading pedagogy in any language should be based on a memory-centered program rather than concentration on sub-skills.

2. *Developing Bicognitive Skills in Children.*

The FI readers in the present study seemed to process printed material in both English and Greek in a manner distinct and more successfully from those readers identified as FD. Hence, once their cognitive style strategies have been ascertained, practice with their less developed strategies should be provided for both groups. Ramirez and Castaneda (1974) argued for bicognitivism (possession of both FD and FI traits) and the development of cognitive flexibility in children by teaching children not only in their preferred mode (matching child's cognitive style to the surrounding environment) but also in an alternative mode (gradually mismatching a child's cognitive style to the environment.) This would enable children to see that there is not only one way to solve a problem or perform a task.

For example, the FD students at the beginning stages of reading, in view of their tendencies toward a global perceptual style, could benefit most in terms of flexibility from an analytic phonics approach in which readers first learn familiar words or sight vocabulary and work with the sounds within them. Obviously, in any reading activity meaning is central but sub-skills can be taught within a meaning-centered reading environment. They could also benefit from a language experience approach (a meaning-centered reading program which uses the students' own dictated stories to provide the content and form of the material read) once the stage of using mediating measures (i.e., phonics) in initial reading instruction is passed.

3. *Importance of a Maintenance Bilingual Program.*

Both the FI and FD groups seem to read with more meaning in English, even though they entered the school speaking very little English and were fluent in Greek. During kindergarten the subjects had equal reading readiness instruction in both languages but by the second grade the subjects were receiving three times as much reading instruction in English. A maintenance bilingual program, instead of the transitional type that existed in the subjects' school, might enable the students to learn English but not at the expense of their native language literacy skills.

Furthermore, the simultaneous teaching of reading in two languages in school's transitional bilingual program may have also adversely affected the development of the subjects' English reading skills (their overall mean grade equivalent score on the California Achievement Test was 3.3 compared to 3.6 for their classmates in the school). Since it was concluded that there seems to be one reading process, it would make sense to teach the reading skills and strategies in the children's stronger language at the time they entered school (in this case, Greek) and transfer the skills and strategies to the second language at a later date, as is the case in maintenance bilingual programs, instead of simultaneously introducing reading instruction in two languages, as is the case in many transitional programs.

REFERENCES

Barrera, R. B. (1978). *Analysis and comparison of the first language and second language oral reading behavior of native Spanish-speaking Mexican American children.* Unpublished doctoral dissertation, The University of Texas at Austin, Texas.

De Silva, A. D. (1978, January). *Oral reading behavior of Spanish-speaking children taught by a meaning based program.* Paper presented at Southwest Education Research Association's Annual Conference, Austin, Texas.

Eaton, A. J. (1978). *A psycholinguistic analysis of the oral reading miscues of selected field-dependent and field-independent native Spanish-speaking Mexican American first-grade children.* Unpublished doctoral dissertation, The University of Texas at Austin, Texas.

Hodes, P. (1976). *A psycholinguistic study of reading miscues of Yiddish-English bilingual children.* Unpublished doctoral dissertation, Wayne State University, Michigan.

Michopoulos, A. (1980). *A language dominance test for Greek bilingual students.* Unpublished doctoral dissertation, Florida State University, Florida.

Mylonas, M. (1981). *Psychological differentiation and biocognitive development among Greek American and Anglo American students in monolingual and bilingual programs.* Unpublished doctoral dissertation, Florida State University, Florida.

Ramirez, M., & Castaneda, A. (1974). *Cultural democracy, biocognitive development and education.* New York: Academic Press.

Smith, F. (1978). *Understanding reading.* New York: Holt, Rinehart & Winston.

Spiridakis, J. (1982). Diagnosing the learning styles of bilingual students and prescribing appropriate instruction. In R. V. Padilla, (Ed.), *Ethnoperspectives in bilingual education: Vol. III* (pp. 307-320). Ypsilanti, Michigan: Eastern Michigan University.

Witkin, H., Dyke, R. B. Faterson, H. F., Goodenough, D. R., & Karp, S. A. (1962). *Psychological differentiation.* New York: Wiley.

Witkin, H., Moore, C., Goodenough, D. R., & Cox, P. (1977). Field dependent and field independent cognitive styles and their educational implications. *Review of Educational Research, 47,* 1-64.

CHAPTER 9

A LANGUAGE DOMINANCE TEST
FOR GREEK AMERICAN
CHILDREN

ARISTOTLE MICHOPOULOS

Interest in the measurement of linguistic proficiency and research in language dominance is a rather recent phenomenon, the largest body of literature in this area appearing during the post-World War II era. Prior to this period, the bulk of language assessment was fused into the verbal aspect of intelligence, aptitude or achievement tests (Anastasi, 1976) and only a small portion of assessment was specifically designed for the assessment of language. If one takes into consideration the multitude of problems related to the creation of an intelligence, achievement or language test for monolinguals, then the magnitude of developing a language test for bilinguals becomes immediately apparent. As William (1971) has pointed out, to create such a test for bilinguals is "doubly complicated because of the interplay of the two languages involved in the experience of the testee" (p. 29).

Two factors that influenced the development of the language tests for bilinguals were the ferment of minority groups in the 1960s (resulting in the Civil Rights Act of 1964) and the public awareness of the particular needs and problems of language-minority children. One of these problems was the inappropriateness of the existing language tests to accurately assess the minority students' knowledge of English and their native language.

This research is based on portions of the author's doctoral dissertation submitted to Florida State University.

151

The most significant factor that affected the development and expansion of language dominance testing was the Supreme Court decision in the *Lau vs. Nichols* case (1974) and related Title VII legislation. The latter made provisions for monetarily penalizing states that were not complying with the legislation or that did not linguistically assess their bilingual student population. For example, the New York City Board of Education had to implement a court-enforced consent decree mandating bilingual testing and teaching for minority children—Spanish-speaking in this case (*Aspira*, 1974)—and, in the case of *Diana vs. California State Education Department* in 1970, "the court decried the misplacement of such students into classes for the mentally retarded based on I.Q. testing in English and has ordered bilingual testing instruments and procedures" (Zirkel, 1974, p. 31).

These cases led to a surge in language assessment and language dominance testing, an undertaking that took various forms, ranging from purely verbal to purely nonverbal assessment. Verbal assessment took the form of interview instruments based on the relative use of both languages at home (Skoczylas, 1971) or the direct measuring of aural-oral performance through questionnaires, story-telling, or question-and-answer strategies (Spolsky et al., 1972). Most of these measures, however, according to Zirkel (1974), "have not proved practicable for educational planning and placement purposes" (p. 35).

The many problems associated with the development of these measures led to the creation of special instruments for planning and placement. Thus, several school districts and publishers have undertaken the development of specialized language dominance instruments for use in bilingual programs, although in some instances valid data have not been utilized in the construction of these instruments. It would be unfair, however, to overlook the great improvement made in such a short time, as well as the quality of some recent tests.

Standardized testing of minority group children resulted in an unfavorable assessment of such children. These discriminatory testing practices resulted in multiple traumas for such children and led to court battles and demands that "compensatory punitive damages" be awarded to plaintiffs in the 1970s. As a result of such battles and the expressed need for reliable instruments, through funding from Department of Health, Education, and Welfare, foundations and publishing firms, many minority language dominance tests were developed in the last decade. The vast majority of these relate to the Spanish-speaking group, while a smaller number addresses the needs of other minority groups.

The rest of this paper will be devoted to the development of such an instrument, the first of its kind, for Greek bilingual children.

TEST DEVELOPMENT

Method

Subjects of the Study

The subjects for the development of the instrument were four hundred and three (403) male and female students attending Grades 1-4 at the Greek Bilingual Program and Greek Parochial School of Tarpon Springs, Florida; the Saint Demetrios Greek Parochial School in New York; the Soterios Ellenas Greek Parochial School in New York; and the Budlong Elementary Public School in Chicago. Criteria used for this selection were locales with a concentration of Greek-speaking people and with the presence of one or more Greek bilingual schools. The selection of these schools and geographic regions is assumed to be representative of Greek bilingual students of the same age in other parts of the country. This procedure of selecting a wide geographical representation enhanced the external validity of the instrument, compared to a selection of limited scope.

Development of the instrument began with a large number of items. Subsequent revisions reduced them to 80 items each for the Greek and English versions (60 pictorial and 20 verbal stimuli). The selection of the initial items was based on a random sampling of words appearing in the vocabulary lists of the Grades 1-4 Readers for Greek and American children. A pool of more than 60 multiple choice items was derived from such vocabulary lists. These items were divided into four general categories aimed at testing the subjects' knowledge of family, neighborhood, school, and church objects. Likewise, more than 20 Greek and English question items were designed to measure the subjects' command of grammar and syntax in each language.

The final instrument consisted of 80 items, 40 for the Greek and 40 for the English text, 30 of which are designed to elicit a response to a verbal stimulus using multiple choice pictorial alternatives. Specifically, each multiple choice item consists of a word stimulus on the left, followed by a series of five related pictures, one of which is the correct answer to the stimulus. The remaining items are verbal stimuli in sentence form designed to elicit a grammatically and syntactically correct answer to a question.

Special care was taken to make the test items reflect the dual history and culture of the subjects. Thus, six items in the multiple choice part of the instrument and two question items differed in the Greek and English components of the tests. The difference reflected the dissimilar sociocultural background of a child raised in Greece as opposed to the U.S.A. For example, item 4 in the multiple choice test depicts a carrot in the English test but an olive in the Greek test, since olives are a much more common item in the Greek diet than carrots; similarly, item 27 depicts the American flag in the English component and the Greek in the Greek.

This general item formulation was presented to 25 raters, who were doctoral students of the Florida State University bilingual program. Many of them were former bilingual teachers and represented such diverse language groups as Greek (eight), Spanish, Tagalog, Vietnamese, and Arabic. The instrument was also presented for feedback to other language specialists and experts at the University and elsewhere.

The experts consulted suggested various changes and/or substitutions in the items and positioning of items within the test. The instrument was revised and again presented to the experts who considered it adequate for its purpose. This examination, critique, revision, and final approval of the instrument was revised and again presented to the experts who considered it adequate for its purpose. This examination, critique, revision, and final approval of the instrument constituted one of the basic steps in establishing its content validity.

After final revision and approval by the panel of reviewers the pictorial test items were given to an illustrator for illustration. After illustrations were completed, the test was finalized in both Greek and English. The test items were placed in a progressive order of difficulty and it was expected that only the students of higher grades would be able to answer most or all of the items correctly.

Selection of the items was based on the following criteria: (a) the items should take cognizance of the child's ability to use such an item at a particular age, (b) the items should be interesting and enjoyable enough to stimulate the child's response, (c) the items should sample a variety of vocabulary and activities, and (d) the items should include, where possible, the same, or similar, or equivalent stimuli in both languages.

Pilot Testing

The Pilot testing included 42 subjects from Grades 1-4 of the Greek Bilingual School and the Church School in Tarpon Springs, Florida. Of these 42 test responses—8 at Grade 1, 10 at Grade 2, 9 at Grade 3, and 15 at Grade 4—two were found invalid and were excluded from computer analyses.

The tests were subsequently coded and given to the Florida State University Evaluation Service Center for a Standard Item Analysis Program. The main statistics of interest in this analysis were the mean, standard deviation, reliability, and standard error of measurement of each group.

Field Testing

Schools and Subjects

After computer analysis of the pilot testing data and ensuing item revision, the instrument was ready for field testing. The field testing included two stages: test and retest. The original number of subjects per grade and school are as follows:

TABLE 1
SUBJECTS BY SCHOOL AND GRADE

Grade	School 1	School 2	School 3	Total
1	23	32	39	94
2	25	37	40	102
3	26	11	55	92
4	16	9	48	73
1-4	90	89	182	361

In order to obtain test-retest data, the instrument was administered twice, with an interval of approximately a week between the two test administrations. Of the 361 subjects tested, only 337 responses were used for computer analysis. The remaining 24 tests were excluded from the analyses, either because they were deemed invalid for various reasons, including "Christmas-treeing," insufficient marking, or reading and writing difficulty (10 cases), or because the subjects were not present in both administrations of the instrument (14 cases). The total number of cases excluded from the analyses is quite small compared to the total sample population. The high rate of clean data is partly attributed to favorable cooperation from the school personnel as well as from the subjects.

Data Coding

The response data were coded onto optically scannable answer sheets. In addition, and prior to this, the writer read and marked all Section B tests, both Greek and English. At the end, each subject had two opscan sheets of data, one for the test and one for the retest.

The data were then separated according to grades and an answer key for each test and section was made. The data were given to the University Evaluation Services so that the appropriate statistical analyses could be made. These analyses included the following: (a) test reliability (co-efficient alpha), (b) mean, standard deviation, and SEM, (c) test-retest reliability, (d) p values per item, (e) point biserial values per item, (e) biserial values per item, and (f) concurrent validity analyses. The analyses were performed for each part and the total of the English and Greek tests, by grade, as well as for the total group of subjects.

Results and Discussion

The results of the study included the following: (a) analysis of the item pool, (b) item selection for final instrument, (c) characteristics of final instrument, (d) test-retest reliabilities, (e) reliabilities by school and sex, and (f) concurrent validity.

Analysis of the Item Pool

The statistical characteristics of the item pool were examined to facilitate selection of items for the final instrument. First, the means and standard deviations of the pupils' scores for each part of the test (Greek and English) were computed. Second, the internal consistency reliability coefficients for the parts were calculated. Third, discrimination indices, correlations between each item and the part score were calculated. The same statistics were calculated for the total 80-item pool. The means, standard deviations, and internal consistency of scores over the items in the pool are shown in Table 2.

TABLE 2
CHARACTERISTICS OF THE ITEM POOL ($N = 302$)

Grade	N	Subtest A			Subtest B			Total Test		
		M	SD	r_{11}	M	SD	r_{11}	M	SD	r_{11}
					English Test					
1	85	35.14	8.45	.876	7.40	5.22	.904	42.54	12.76	.927
2	61	38.60	5.62	.765	11.67	4.09	.862	50.27	8.72	.868
3	87	43.87	8.46	.913	14.15	3.83	.846	58.39	10.81	.927
4	69	39.48	4.89	.772	16.97	3.19	.838	56.45	7.04	.853
1-4	302	43.10	8.61	.901	12.57	5.51	.921	55.66	13.20	.941
					Greek Test					
1	85	32.45	13.60	.947	4.93	4.56	.898	37.38	16.67	.955
2	61	42.33	8.81	.890	7.73	4.24	.849	50.07	11.50	.911
3	87	43.03	10.16	.923	10.80	4.20	.821	53.84	12.81	.930
4	69	44.17	10.25	.930	12.26	5.01	.904	56.43	14.36	.951
1-4	302	40.11	12.04	.941	9.04	5.32	.904	49.15	16.05	.954

The data show that the mean performance of subjects was greater on the English items than on the Greek items. Since the content of the items was designed to be parallel, this difference in performance is probably due to greater competence of the subjects in the English language, which is the primary language in the subjects' schools. Subjects were more variable in their performance on the Greek items than the English items. This finding might be associated with the difference in means and a slight tendency toward ceiling effects. For example, the largest standard deviation is associated with the smallest mean for total scores on both the English and Greek tests. The items have a substantial degree of internal consistency as reflected in the alpha coefficients.

Item Selection for Final Instrument

In examining the data for internal consistency, item and part analyses showed that the 80-item pool possessed the appropriate statistical characteristics to permit development of a shorter instrument. The final instrument included 40 Greek and 40 English items. Specifically, the selection of the 40 items (30 multiple choice and 10 free-response items) was based on the following criteria: (a) each item should have an acceptable point biserial value (greater than or equal to .30), (b) the parts (English and Greek) of the instrument should be based, item by item, on the same pictorial or question clues, (c) the two parts of the final instrument should possess the closest possible point biserial values, item by item, and items whose Greek or English components might present significantly different point biserial values should be excluded, and (d) the resulting Greek and English parts of the final instrument should present comparable reliabilities. Thus, the final parts of the instrument were designed to be of equal difficulty for a balanced bilingual child.

All items without variance were automatically excluded from consideration in the final selection process. Furthermore, the selection of an item was based on its overall performance and not merely on its performance in selected grades. Based on the foregoing criteria, 40 items were finally selected for both the Greek and English parts of the instrument.

Characteristics of Final Instrument

Reliabilities and other pertinent statistics obtained by the final 40-item instrument are presented in Table 3.

TABLE 3
STATISTICAL CHARACTERISTICS OF THE FINAL 40-ITEM INSTRUMENT BY GRADE LEVEL AND OVERALL

Gr.	N	English Test				Greek Test				Differences between the Two Parts			
		M	SD	r_{11}	SEM	M	SD	r_{11}	SEM	M	SD	r_{11}	SEM
1	85	23.10	8.04	.910	2.41	20.15	9.93	.936	2.38	2.95	8.25	.830	3.38
2	61	30.15	5.70	.843	2.28	28.05	6.62	.865	2.38	2.10	8.13	.840	3.25
3	87	33.98	5.10	.863	1.89	29.27	7.30	.895	2.34	4.70	8.37	.870	3.01
4	69	34.09	4.00	.776	1.92	30.06	8.01	.922	2.24	4.03	7.75	.850	3.02
1-4	302	30.49	7.80	.924	2.18	26.50	9.10	.931	2.37	3.99	8.22	.840	3.29

TABLE 4
TEST-RETEST RELIABILITIES BY GRADE LEVEL AND OVERALL

Gr.		N	English Part					Greek Part					Differences between the Two Parts			
				M	SD	r_{11}	SEM		M	SD	r_{11}	SEM		M	SD	r_{11}	SEM
1	E1	85		23.10	8.04	.715	2.41	G1	20.15	9.93	.754	2.38	D1	2.95	8.25	.686	3.38
	E2			22.86	8.44		4.47	G2	19.59	9.59		4.80	D2	3.27	7.58		4.24
2	E1	61		30.15	5.70	.863	2.28	G1	28.05	6.62	.821	2.38	D1	2.10	8.13	.860	3.25
	E2			29.75	6.27		2.32	G2	27.58	7.09		2.98	D2	2.17	7.89		2.92
3	E1	87		33.98	5.10	.822	1.89	G1	29.27	7.30	.476	2.34	D1	4.70	8.37	.572	3.01
	E2			33.20	5.34		2.24	G2	28.73	7.39		5.39	D2	4.47	9.06		5.98
4	E1	69		34.09	4.00	.661	1.92	G1	30.06	8.01	.888	2.24	D1	4.03	7.75	.861	3.02
	E2			35.01	4.09		2.37	G2	28.48	9.50		3.14	D2	6.54	8.50		3.15
1-4	E1	302		30.40	7.80	.853	2.18	G1	26.50	9.10	.781	2.37	D1	3.99	8.22	.728	3.29
	E2			29.90	7.96		3.10	G2	25.78	9.37		4.40	D2	4.12	8.38		4.36

The reliabilities on both the Greek and English parts of the instrument are quite high and only slightly lower than those of the entire item pool (see Table 2). The differences between the reliabilities of the two parts of the instrument are negligible and are not statistically significant. The largest difference appears in Grade 4, where the reliabilties were .78 for the English part and .92 for the Greek part. This difference may be attributed to a low variance and high mean for the English part for this grade which may have caused a ceiling effect, as well as to a restriction in the sample compilation since the majority of subjects for this grade (47 out of 69) came from the same school. However, the difference between the two reliabilities is not statistically significant.

As shown in Table 3, means for the Greek and English parts are consistently different. This difference, which favors the English part and is larger on the higher grades, is statistically significant and indicates a greater competence of the subjects in the English language.

The standard deviations of the instrument are generally high compared to those of the 80-items pool (see Table 2), since all items excluded from the final instrument had low or no variance and thus their exclusion had no serious effect on the variability of the instrument. The standard deviations of the Greek part are generally higher than those of the English. These higher standards deviations and accompanying larger variances are the basic reason for the higher reliabilities of the Greek part, since there is a direct relationship between these two statistics. The Grade 4 standard deviation of the Greek part is higher than expected, especially when compared to the standard deviations of Grades 2 and 3. The reason for this high standard deviation may be due to a wide variability in language ability among the subjects of this group.

The standard errors of measurement for both parts are comparably small. These small standard errors of measurement are also reflected in the generally high reliabilities of both parts, since there is an inverse relationship between these two statistics.

The reliabilities of the difference between scores on the English and Greek parts are quite large and stable across grade levels. These values are quite satisfying, because it is the difference between the scores on the English and Greek parts that constitutes the language dominance score. Therefore, these reliabilities are crucial to the effectiveness of the instrument in reliability differentiating between Greek and English dominant children.

The remaining statistics for the differences, means, standard deviations, and standard errors of measurement are also stable. The standard error of measurement values are higher than those of each individual part because the variances of errors of measurement are added together when the difference between parts is determined.

Test-Retest Reliabilities

The instrument was administered a second time to the subjects, approximately one week after the first administration, to examine the stability of its results over a period of time. Table 4 shows three test-retest reliability results by grade level and overall.

The test-retest reliabilities, with the exception of Grade 3 of the Greek part, showed considerable stability of results over time. Additionally, test-retest reliabilities of the difference between the two parts of the instrument are substantial.

Considering the numerous sources of error that can enter into a test-retest administration as compared to a single ad--ministration of an instrument, the obtained overall reliabilities of .85 for the English part and .78 for the Greek seem adequately large. The reliabilities of the differences between the English and Greek parts are especially encouraging in view of the difficulties often associated with the use of indices generated from the difference between two scores.

Reliabilities by School

Table 5, which summarizes the reliabilities of the instrument by school shows that reliabilities were acceptably high both for individual schools as well as overall. Additionally, the reliabilities of the differences between the two parts by individual school and overall are extremely close. The means of the two components are very similar for school 1, but they are higher for the English part in school 3 and especially school 2, denoting that the subjects of schools 3 and 2 had greater competence in English. This is explained by the fact that school 1 is a public school with a large variability of ability among its subjects—many of which are recent Greek immigrant children—while schools 3 and 2 are parochial with a more homogeneous, "Americanized" middle class student population. The means of the difference between the two parts expresses the numerical difference between the English and Greek parts of the instrument and the higher scoring of the subjects, especially in school 2, on the English part.

Finally, the standard deviations of the difference are stable and large across schools. The standard errors of measurement are almost identical among schools, showing that the instrument's performance was similar among schools. This similarity, along with similarities among the standard deviations and reliabilities, show the good performance of the instrument among different school settings.

Reliabilities by Sex

Sex as a variable did not appear to have an effect on the reliability of the instrument. Table 6 shows the similar reliability values yielded for females and males on both English (.917 vs. .923) and Greek (.925 vs. .942) parts. The table also indicates that the standard error of measurement values for males and females are small on both parts.

The tests yielded slightly higher standard deviation values for males, especially on the Greek component, resulting in slightly higher but not, statistically, significantly different reliability values for males when compared to females.

A difference of means in favor of the female subjects is shown, which is statistically significant on both the English and Greek parts at the $p < .05$ level. The yield of higher scores for female subjects coincides with research findings (Restak, 1979) on sex as a predictor of language acquisition.

In the reliability of difference values between the two parts, a difference, not statistically significant, is shown in favor of the males —.88 vs. .78. This difference may be attributed to the larger standard deviation of the scores of the males.

Concurrent Validity

Content validity of the instrument was established through a panel of experts. To further investigate the validity

TABLE 5
RELIABILITIES OF THE FINAL INSTRUMENT BY SCHOOL(S)

Sch.	N	English				Greek				Differences between the Two Parts			
		M	SD	r_{11}	SEM	M	SD	r_{11}	SEM	M	SD	r_{11}	SEM
1	79	26.31	9.46	.935	2.27	25.99	10.12	.952	2.23	.32	8.45	.850	3.30
2	48	26.89	9.10	.941	2.18	19.30	10.72	.952	2.36	7.59	10.06	.900	3.22
3	175	33.21	5.30	.847	2.07	28.34	7.19	.889	2.37	4.87	6.64	.770	3.19
1-3	302	30.49	7.80	.924	2.18	26.50	9.10	.931	2.37	3.99	8.22	.840	3.29

TABLE 6
RELIABILITIES BY SEX

Sex Gr.	N	English				Greek				Difference between the Two Parts			
		M	SD	r_{11}	SEM	M	SEM	r_{11}	SEM	M	SD	r_{11}	SEM
M 1-4	138	29.56	8.27	.923	2.32	24.62	10.03	.942	2.41	4.94	9.53	.880	3.34
F 1-4	164	31.12	7.57	.917	2.12	27.71	8.17	.925	2.12	3.41	6.62	.780	3.11

of the instrument, however, an examination of its concurrent validity was undertaken. Teacher ratings of the bilingualism of each student were used as an independent criterion measure of language dominance. Each subject was assigned a code reflecting his/her language classification as designated by the teachers; a code of 1 indicated Greek language dominance, a code of 2 indicated balanced bilingualism, and a code of 3 indicated English language dominance. The teacher ratings were transferred to the subjects' computer record and a correlation coefficient expressing the teacher/instrument agreement was obtained.

Such correlations are usually low due to the multiple sources of error entering their calculation. Sources of error may arise from a teacher's subjective evaluation of a subject's bilingualism. Such errors may be based on factors such as the length of acquaintance with the subject, teaching experience, teacher's degree of bilingualism, and subject's foreign accent or lack of it, resulting in leniency error, halo effect error, and so on. Such errors increase the likelihood of misclassification of a subject. Another important factor which contributes to the misclassification of a subject is the category of balanced bilinguals, but also bilinguals with a leaning towards one language. The extent of this leaning is quite difficult to ascertain and is therefore an important potential source of error. Finally, the imperfection of the instrument per se contributes to error.

The concurrent validity coefficients for this study were obtained in the following way. First, the Greek and English scores for each subject were calculated and the Greek score was subtracted from the English score. Second, the subjects were classified as Greek dominant, balanced bilingual, or English dominant based on the difference calculated in the first step. A subject was classified as Greek or English dominant if the difference between his or her Greek and English scores was larger than approximately + or − 1.5 standard errors of measurement, or + or − 5 points. If the score difference was smaller than the mentioned error of measurement difference, the subject was classified as a balanced bilingual. The selection of this value for the classification of the subjects was arrived at through a process of professional judgement and examination of the data.

The resulting classifications of subjects were then compared to the teacher ratings. The correlation coefficients obtained per grade and overall were as follows: Grade 1, .47; Grade 2, .47; Grade 3, .56; Grade 4, .27; and Grades 1-4, .47.

CONCLUSION

The instrument developed filled a gap in the area of language dominance testing for the Greek bilingual children. Examinations of the instrument in relation to field-test data, internal consistency reliability, test-retest reliability, reliability by school and sex, and validity demonstrated that the instrument possessed high reliability and satisfactory validity values. Furthermore, the data from the instrument were consistent with existing theories about the relationship between the language ability of subjects of different socioeconomic backgrounds.

Beyond the purely abstract information the data collected shed light on some other aspects of student and parent attitudes and values. For example, in a cursory examination of the students' answers regarding the country that they would like to visit the most, Greece is by far their first choice—even when they do not know how to spell it correctly!—with Italy and England as poor seconds. On the question of how they celebrate their birthday, the answer shows a rather typical American environment, i.e. "cake and cokes!" Regarding their favorite shows, "The Incredible Hulk" seemed to enchant the boys, while "Happy Days" scored very high among the girls! Coming to spending patterns, it seems that we are dealing here with the "good old value" of frugality. Thus the number one answer to the question: "What would you do, if you had a lot of money?", was: "I would put it in the bank." A few ventured buying a home and some boys thought of buying a "κάρο." If we accept the wisdom of the Modern Greek saying "κατά μάνα κατά τάτα, κατά γιὸ καὶ θυγατέρα," or the simpler American "like father, like son," then, we can safely deduce that the Greek-American children reflect the values of their parents, who believe in hard work and saving, love for the country of their origin and high value on education. This last one is further evidenced by the higher scores of students attending parochial than public schools. Their scores were certainly higher than their fellow-students attending public schools.

Another expected finding was that the students were more

competent in English than Greek. Similarly, as the teachers already know the girls possess a better language aptitude than the boys, who in turn take their "revenge" by showing better stability on their scores than the girls.

One final and very interesting finding for this writer and many teachers and parents, I presume, was a very ingenious approach to school attendance by the students. Here both girls and boys agree and if the Board of Education and the citizens would listen to their advice their Tax Bill would be substantially lower. To be more specific, when they were asked: "How many days per week would you like to go to school, if you had your choice?", their most favorite answer was the number three! And here I hope that the answer does not reflect the values of their parents!

REFERENCES

Anastasi, A. (1976). *Psychological testing*. (4th ed.). New York: Macmillan.

Aspira, Inc. v. Board of Education, No. 72 Civ. 4002 MEF (S.D. N.Y., September 20, 1974).

Diana v. California State Education Department, C.A. No. C-7037 RFD (N.D. Cal., February 3, 1970).

Restak, R. M. (1979). *The brain: The last frontier*. New York: Doubleday & Company, Inc.

Skoczylas, R. (1971). Home bilingual usage estimate. Gilroy, California: Copywritten instrument.

Spolsky, B| et al. (1972). Three functional tests of language proficiency. *TESOL Quarterly, 6*, 221-235.

William, C. (1971). The construction of standardized tests for Welshspeaking children. *Educational Research, 14*, 29-31.

Zirkel, P. A. (1974). *Modular sequence: Teaching reading to bilingual learners*. West Hartford, Connecticut: Hartford University. (ERIC Document Reproduction Service No. ED 106 239 (b)).

CHAPTER 10

SEX EDUCATION
AND GREEK AMERICANS

MARY P. LEFKARITES

This paper begins with a description of a workshop experience that took place as part of the conference on Education and Greek Americans: Process and Prospects (Orfanos & Psomiades, 1986). The workshop description is followed by a discussion of an issue that is central to the lives of Greek Americans—sex education and their children. Included in this discussion is a point of view that addresses the need for introducing sex education into the Greek American school system and a description of a model program in family life education.

The Workshop Experience

On the final afternoon of the conference, a group of twenty-one Greek American professionals signed up for a workshop designed to explore the theme of sex education. Having been involved in teaching sexuality courses at Hunter College for the past 15 years of my life, I could sense the tension within the group as we gathered together for this unique cultural experience.

The session began with the participants completing a written questionnaire that included data on gender, age, place of birth, place of schooling, and whether schooling was private or public. Other questions addressed the source from which most of their education about sex came, the nature of that information, who they could go to regarding questions on sex, and what feelings were conveyed to them in the family about sexual matters. In addition, the questionnaire addressed what gender differences existed in the family among those individuals who grew up with a sibling of the opposite gender, and whether participants felt that sex education belongs in a school curriculum.

The group consisted of seven men and fourteen women with an age range between 25-58 among those individuals who reported their age. More than half of the participants were born and received their primary education in the United States. Less than one-third of the entire group had any formal education on sexuality in school and, of those who did, most received this education on the high school level.

While the group was small, gender differences were evident in the data that participants provided. One distinction concerns sources of "education" about sex. Sources among all participants included parents, sibling, other relatives, friends, partners, books/magazines, television/movies and formal education. The primary sources for men came from friends. Books and magazines as well as partners were a second source. The primary source for women was books and magazines with friends providing a second source of information. More than half of the women received some information from a parent who, with one exception, was a mother. In contrast, none of the men received information from either parent.

Sources that participants felt they could go to regarding questions on sex included friends, books, mothers, sisters, other relatives, and partners. One of the limitations of this question is that there was no way of ascertaining at what age participants felt they could approach these sources. It may be that in earlier childhood and adolescence, more people would have had fewer sources. In any case, responses indicated that for both men and women, friends were the most likely individuals they could approach. Books were the second most likely source. Three women identified a parent, mothers in all three cases. None of the men identified either parent. Two women stated that there was no one they could approach.

Both men and women indicated that similar feelings were conveyed in their families regarding sexual matters. The overwhelming response was that of a negative nature. These responses included the following:

"It was something good girls do not do. (You) don't talk about it."[1]

"A subject (that was) not to be approached or discussed."

"Fear of sex."

"Restrained. Secretive."

"That it was taboo—something not to be discussed."

"Very private and not to be discussed explicitly—only vague references."

"That sex was something to be avoided in discussion."

"We didn't discuss it."

"Secretive, not to be discussed at length."

"Sex was unheard (of)."

"It's forbidden."

"When (the) subject arose, (there were) feelings of discomfort about its discussion."

"Sexual matters were private and not to be discussed by my mother."

"Not to be spoken of."

"Negative."

"None. Some taboos surfaced in discussions. But sex knowledge would eventually come."

"Taboo."

"Joking and anxiety. Sex was never really spoken of openly."

"Sex did not exist—my mother was a virgin, my sister and I just happened along. Sex was never/is never discussed."

"It's not for fun; religion; morality."

In only one case a younger woman participant disclosed that "open and comfortable feelings" were conveyed in her family.

[1]Italics are those of the author for clarification.

Different treatment of opposite sex sibling was apparent among those participants who grew up with sibling of the opposite gender. These differences were expressed more frequently by women. Four of seven women who grew up with brothers reported some differences. Their responses were as follows:

"Double standards."

"Yes—had to do the housework, could not go out."

"Yes—more restrictions."

"Yes—household tasks were women's work."

A fifth woman initially responded with "no" but added, "there were however more restrictions for me as to dating."

Among five men who grew up with sisters, two expressed differences in treatment. Their responses were:

"Yes. I was given more freedom. Sex, while not spoken about, was O.K. for me but not for my sister."

"There was an implicit assumption that I could be/ would be sexual and that my sister would not know about sex let alone participate in sex."

A third man's response was "not noticeable." This man's response suggests that gender differences may be more common than thought but not perceived by opposite sex sibling.

The consensus among all participants concerning whether sex education belongs in the school curriculum was affirmative. Some individuals qualified their responses which included:

"If tastefully or, should I say, diplomatically handled."

"Within (the) context of family life education."

"But it should be given by a specialist such as a medical doctor, psychologist, etc."

Once the questionnaire was completed, I asked the participants to form three different groups with one group consisting of all the men who were present. Within each group, participants were asked to share whatever information they felt comfortable disclosing on the questionnaire. We then opened into one large group and reporters for each group summarized their discussion. Apparently, people conveyed much more information on their socialization within their small group discussions than what was requested of them. Large group discussions focused on gender differences concerning sexuality. Some individuals experienced more liberal upbringings concerning information and nudity within the family. However, these experiences were exceptions to the traditional patterns that existed among most participants. Other questions were explored in the larger group and included a definition of sex education and when it should begin, the role of parents regarding the sex education of their children, and issues that may arise in the classroom regarding children's sexuality as well as how to deal with them.

As facilitator of the group, I sensed an eagerness among people in the workshop to talk with and listen to each other once the level of anxiety was reduced. In the small groups, this was conveyed in the interactions of people with each other and sharing of information that went beyond that which was requested of them. In the large group, participants were eager to hear of opposite gender socialization experiences regarding sexuality. At the end of the session, many individuals conveyed their appreciation and satisfaction in having been able to participate in this learning experience.

A Clarification of Sex Education and Sexuality

Patterns that became apparent from the written questionnaire and discussion among this small group of Greek Americans are consistent with the socialization of boys and girls in the United States regarding their sexuality. Parents are *not* the primary source of sex information for young people. Most adolescents would like to talk with parents but turn to peers as their primary source. When sex information is provided in the home, mothers are the source for both girls and boys. Unfortunately, parents lack the knowledge and skill to actively and positively educate their children. Consequently, they feel uncomfortable in carrying out this important aspect of parenting. At the same time, most parents (79%) favor sex education in schools (Cook, Kirby, Wilson, and Alter, 1984).

This raises questions that we addressed in our group. What is sex education? When does it begin? Most individuals mistakenly equate sex education with learning about sex facts and sexual intercourse. This is a narrow and erroneous view of sex education. A broader definition includes both verbal and non-verbal messages that are conveyed to us the moment we are born—the way we are held, cooed to, dressed; the toys with which we are permitted to play; messages parents convey to us about our genitalia and body; expectations placed on us because of our gender in the home, school, church and other settings in our life; the manner in which our parents communicate with each other; the roles our parents have at home, work and other settings; and, gender images we are presented with in mass media. These are all examples of sex education.

Within this frame of reference, children are constantly being "sex educated," often, unfortunately in negative ways. As was indicated in the responses of participants in the workshop, parents, with the best interest at heart for their children, most often communicate negative verbal and nonverbal messages—"don't!" Silence is another powerful message. Different role expectations are placed on boys and girls, many of which are damaging to self-esteem and adult interpersonal relations. Peers misinform and pressure each other to be sexually active (Strong and Reynolds, 1983).

Media—television, videos, radio, recordings, films, magazines, and advertisements—constantly inform young people that they should be sexy, sexually active, sexually active with many partners, and spontaneous in their sexual relations. (The recent publicity concerning the AIDS crisis is beginning to alter these messages.) Media also transmits some very destructive gender messages: women as degraded objects; men as super studs who are as sexually potent as the material success they are supposed to attain; and, sex as an act associated with violence. Children are the latest target of exploitation by media. While there has not been any substantial research associating media exposure with behavior, the long term effects of this exposure are unknown.

Associated with clarifying what ,'sex education" means is the broader concept of sexuality. As with sex education, genital sex is the first association made with this concept. The Sex Information and Education Council of the United States (SIECUS) (Carrera and Calderone, 1980) has developed a definition which I feel explains the meaning of sexuality and one that I share with my college classes. It is as follows:

> The SIECUS concept of sexuality refers to the totality of being a person. It includes all of those aspects of the human being that relate specifically to being boy or girl, woman or man, and is an entity subject to life-long dynamic change. Sexuality reflects our human character, not solely our genital nature. As a function of the total personality it is concerned with the biological, psychological, sociological, spiritual, and cultural variables of life which, by their effects on personality development and interpersonal relations, can in turn affect social structure.

Clearly, this concept of sexuality encompasses all aspects of one's life including the cultural and spiritual.

Family Life Education in Schools

There are a number of concerns that are raised regarding the teaching of sexuality in a school setting. Those concerns most often voiced by parents include whether a program will encourage sexual activity and replace family, religious, and cultural values. Parents also want to know if a program will be taught by qualified individuals. These are all legitimate concerns of parents that need to be addressed.

One of the most important aspects of developing and implementing a school sex education program is to involve parents in that process. This involvement includes their full knowledge and understanding of the program as well as their active contributions in developing the curriculum. A process that encourages their participation will not only provide a means for sensitizing and educating them but will also serve to gain their support for the program.

The concerns of parents can be addressed by looking at the content of existing programs in the United States. One example is the Kindergarten through Grade 12 Family Life Education Curriculum written by the staff of Planned Parenthood of Northern New England (1983). I shared this curriculum with members of the General Secretariat on the Equality of the Sexes in Athens last August while working on a proposal for introducing sex education in the public school system of Greece. The Planned Parenthood Family Life Education Curriculum is a comprehensive curriculum that builds on concepts from one year to the next within the context of human developmental stages. Content areas of the curriculum focus on gender messages, body images, family roles, affection and intimacy, and learning about sexual intercourse as well as its consequences. It is intended to help young people communicate more effectively with their parents, resist peer pressure and media messages regarding sexual behavior, delay in having first intercourse, and to prepare them in using contraception when they do become sexually active.

There are other broader intentions. One of these intentions is to help young people resist sexual exploitation by others and to relieve them of the need to exploit others by helping them gain confidence in the sexual dimension of their lives. It is intended to help them make responsible decisions about sexual matters and to prepare them for long-term relationships through learning activities on communication and the meaning of life. Another intention is to help them accept and respect lifestyle choices of others that are different from their own.

Topics for the different grade levels are listed in this section to provide an overview of content areas based on the age of the students. Included among these topics are preventative sexual abuse lessons which have been identified as "personal safety" lessons. They are listed separately at the end of various grade level topics and can be integrated among other lessons.

Topics by Grade Level

KINDERGARTEN (NURSERY)

1. Families come in all shapes and sizes.
2. Families change in different ways.
3. Family members work together and are courteous of one another.
4. Girls and boys are alike in many ways and different in a few others.
5. Friends are important people.
6. We make decisions for ourselves all the time.

Personal Safety:

1. Feeling good about yourself is an important feeling.
2. You are special and also like everybody else.
3. People have feelings which affect how we feel about ourselves physically and emotionally.
4. Keeping your body safe. (This includes the concept that: body parts are private; there are different types of touch, some which are good, others that are negative).

GRADE 1

1. Family member help one another in many different ways. (This includes the concept that mothers and fathers share jobs inside and outside the home.)
2. Developing support systems.
3. Families grow and change all the time. (Lessons focus on where babies come from, where they grow, how they are born, and what needs they have.)
4. Every person has special qualities which make one unique.
5. Friendships.
6. We have to make choices when we make decisions.

GRADE 2

1. There are many different kinds of families in our community. Families help meet our basic needs.
2. Familiy members must work together to get their work done.
3. One of the many ways families grow and change is by adding members through adoption or foster care.
4. Growing up means more than getting bigger.
5. Expressing our feelings.
6. As we grow up, we accept more responsibility and get more privileges.
7. Respecting another person's property.
8. Advertisers see children as consumers.

GRADE 3

1. Our family is larger than just the people who live in our house.
2. A family works together so they can enjoy one another.
3. Learning to get along with brothers and sisters helps to teach us how to get along with people.
4. A family goes through changes when a member leaves.
5. We developed from two adult humans. (This topic includes facts concerning the male/female reproductive and sexual system and that "a man puts his penis into a woman's vagina and deposits sperm.")
6. Expressing angry feelings.
7. Males and females have similar abilities and can do similar things.
8. How we feel about ourselves shapes how we behave, get along with others and act toward others.
9. We can follow some simple steps when making decisions.

Personal Safety—Grades 1-3:

1. Our support system can help with a problem.
2. Identifying safe and unsafe requests.
3. Assertiveness can help avoid dangerous situations.
4. Children can avoid or stop dangerous situations.
5. Building self-esteem can help avoid victimization.
6. Your body is your own. We each have needs for privacy.
7. Having friendships and taking care of our things is a lesson in respect.
8. Senses give us information about what we like and don't like.
9. Senses can alert us to possible danger.
10. Definitions of sexual abuse, protection strategies, and the importance of telling.
11. Touches can be good, bad, and confusing.

GRADE 4

1. People in families many times resemble one another.
2. Family communication/family meetings.

3. Each person in a family has to adjust when the family moves to a different community.
4. How you came to be—fertilization and heredity.
5. Feeling good about ourselves is essential to our mental well-being.
6. Sex role expectations.
7. How do you choose friends.
8. Sometimes we make decisions because of what others think.

GRADE 5

1. Where you are born in your family (1st child, 2nd child, etc.) can have an affect on your relationships. (This topic includes: "Are sons and daughters treated differently in families? How are they treated the same?")
2. Family communications: when we understand our parents' concerns, we can understand their reactions better.
3. When one member of the family has a problem/illness, all other family members are affected too.
4. The reproductive systems in the human begin to work. (This topic includes facts concerning the menstrual cycle.)
5. Puberty is a time of rapid growth and development in our lives. (Male and female external genitalia are included in this topic. Teachers are advised at this point to set up a question box in a heavily used area of the classroom where students may drop off anonymous questions.)
6. Most people wish they could change things about themselves.
7. Stereotypes may be helpful or harmful in getting to know people.
8. Many times our behavior is affected by people we know. (This topic includes discussion on peer pressure.)
9. Television shows, and advertisements can be evaluated for not-so-obvious messages.

GRADE 6

1. Family members grow up with rituals they share with one another.
2. While we are experiencing changes in our physical and

emotional development, our parents are growing and changing too.

3. As we reach puberty, our body functions change and affect more than our reproductive systems. (This topic includes recognition that sexual feelings of both females and males are normal.)
4. Believing in ourselves is basic to feeling good about ourselves.
5. Needing to be part of a group can sometimes cause people to do things they would not normally think was O.K. (This topic focuses on peers and peer pressure.)
6. Developing friendships with males and females.
7. At any one time, many people may have an effect on what decisions we make.

GRADE 7

1. The family's roles in society change as society changes but the roles of maintenance of all members and child-rearing continues.
2. As family members grow and change, their rights and responsibilities increase too. (This topic includes sex role differences regarding rights and privileges.)
3. It is common for children and parents to disagree on how many freedoms and responsibilities a young person should have.
4. Knowing how and taking care of yourself is one of the ways adults know we are ready for further responsibilities. (This topic focuses on healthy grooming habits including products sold to females regarding menstruation and vaginal "odors.")
5. Breast self-exam and testicular self-exam are health habits that are part of taking care of ourselves.
6. Our physical characteristics may cause us pride or pain.
7. Planning for the future helps people prepare themselves by setting goals.
8. Boys and girls may have misconceptions about one another that may interfere with relationships.
9. Many people can provide information and advice on interpersonal relationships.

GRADE 8

1. Our parents' perspectives on life may be based on what they have experienced in their lives. (This topic includes discussions of events that have radically changed family life such as, the automobile, computers, medical technology, roles of females, and media.)
2. Family members are affected by the behavior and accomplishments of other family members.
3. Caring for others is part of the responsibilities of a mature family member. (This topic focuses on child care.)
4. Most males and females in this age are physically capable of producing a pregnancy. (This includes facts on ovulation, male ejaculation, intercourse, fertilization and implantation.)
5. Pregnancy can be avoided by not having intercourse, or by using contraception. (This topic includes the male's responsibility as well as the female's in avoiding pregnancy, and methods of birth control as well as where to obtain them.)
6. How we feel about ourselves (self-concept) affects our behavior with others.
7. Investigating career options expands one's future job posibilities.
8. Deciding how much responsibility we have for our friends is an issue we will grapple with throughout our lives.
9. Dating usually presents many dilemmas for young people.
10. The decision to engage in sexual intercourse involves many decisions. (The content of this topic includes the fact that in the United States 87% of 13 year old boys and 98% of 13 year old girls have *not* had sex.

Personal Safety—Grades 7 and 8:

1. Introduction to the concept of sexual abuse and exploitation: facts and myths, including date rape.
2. Vulnerability, tricks and traps, importance of telling, types of touch.
3. Touch and protection rules.
4. Practicing assertive responses/summarizing previous learning.

GRADES 9-12

Reproductive Health:

1. Knowledge of our reproductive system can aid decision making about our health behavior and about appropriate times to seek health care. (This topic includes male anatomy and health care as well as community resources that assist with sexual health care needs.)
2. Recognizing normal and abnormal symptoms of the reproductive system can assist people in managing their health care. (This topic includes female anatomy and sexual health care as well as community resources assisting with sexual health care needs.)
3. Understanding the menstrual cycle can relieve anxiety about normal body functioning.
4. Knowledge of the various contraceptive methods can aid a person in making decision about her/his sexual activity. (This topic includes the possible outcomes of sexual activity, community resources for birth control, and the option of waiting until marriage.)
5. Pregnancy and parenthood involve major life changes which affect both physical health and lifestyle. (This topic includes informed pregnancy, childbirth and parenthood for seeking appropriate care when and if the time comes.)
6. Teenage pregnancy carries many risks and requires making the decision of whether to keep the pregnancy, relinquish the baby for adoption, or terminate the pregnancy. (This topic includes legal rights and responsibilities for each alternative as well as clarification and expression of values concerning alternatives.)

Interpersonal Relationships/Friendships:

1. Friendships frequently become less valued as dating relationships begin to take prominence in one's life.
2. Same-sex relationships among adolescents offer support and caring from peers which can last for years. Fear of homosexual relationships, or fear of appearing to be homosexual, may impede the development of positive same sex relationships.

3. Dating is a social phenomenon in our culture which carries traditions and expectations.
4. Applying the decision making model to interpersonal dilemmas can help sort out difficult situations. (A process for making decisions as well as consideration for family and personal values is included in learning strategies.)
5. The role and timing of love and intercourse within a dating relationship pose concern for many adolescents. (This topic includes the pros and cons of being sexually active as well as how sex is used and distinctions between love and infatuation.)
6. Sex role stereotypes are being challenged continuously, necessitating adaptability both at home and at work.

Family—Decisions About Parenthood:

1. The decision to become a parent requires an understanding of tasks and skills necessary for parenthood. (This topic is coordinated with the Reproductive Health topic of "Pregnancy and Childbirth." It focuses on communication skills for raising children, if one chooses to parent, in a positive context by including issues such as, problem solving, developing alternatives to punishment, giving praise and building self-esteem, freeing people from labels, reflective listening, and engaging cooperation.)
2. Family dynamics change dramatically as all members age and mature.

Personal Safety:

1. Introduction to Sexual Abuse and Exploitation: facts and myths.
2. Vulnerability, Trusting Our Feelings, Telling Others/ Getting Help, Types of Touch.
3. Protection Rules. (This topic includes asserting one's boundaries.)
4. Practicing assertive responses/summarizing previous learning about non-consenting situations.

Clearly, this curriculum is not one that condones sex activity at a young age but one that is intended to prepare young people for healthier adult relations that include love, responsibility, intimacy, care, positive self-image, equality between the genders as well as responsible parenting. It is also intended to prevent the consequences of early sexual activity and sexual exploitation.

The New York City Curriculum for Kindergarten through Grade 12 (New York City Board of Education, 1985) and other curricula throughout the United States are similar to that of Planned Parenthood of Northern New England. They provide young people with the opportunity to attain the knowledge, motivation and capabilities necessary for responsible decision-making and to help prepare them deal effectively with the responsibilities of family life, marriage, parenting, and social relations. Unfortunately, less than 10% of youngsters throughout the United States participate in a comprehensive class that lasts at the minimum, 40 hours (Cook, Kirby, Wilson, and Alter, 1984).

Regarding the issue of who is qualified to teach sex education, the backgrounds of sex education teachers vary in the United States. Health education, health and physical education, home economics, and biology are some of the more common specializations from which they come. Some have had special training in sex education while others have not.

Colleges are increasingly adding courses to their curricula for this purpose. In the state of Michigan, 6 semester hours in the biological or behavioral sciences are prescribed in addition to 2 hours in health education and 2 hours (plus 20 inservice hours) in sex education (Dickman, 1984). In a program that I coordinate at Hunter College, school health education majors are required to take a 3 credit sex education course, two methodolgy courses in which approaches to teaching sex education are included, and two additional courses that expose students to sex education curricula. These majors are trained to teach in junior and senior high schools.

In addition to formal study courses on the university level, some teachers are trained through in-service programs while others receive both formal and in-service training. Another option is preparation through a continuing education program.

Guidelines for the selection of potential sex educators have been identified by individuals in the field of sexuality who have gathered information and conducted research in this area. Teacher selection includes an individual who supports the basic values of the community and his/her society, is committed to supporting parents as the primary sex educators of their children, and is able to gain and keep the trust of her/his administrator and community. More specific qualifications concern genuine enthusiasm about teaching sex education, participation in human sexuality workshops or courses, understanding and appreciation of what it is like to be an adolescent, and a clear understanding of the basic values of her/his society.

Other skills that are considered essential include the ability to effectively handle potentially sensitive questions or situations, the ability to keep individual sexual concerns or feelings from affecting classroom instruction, the ability to create an environment conducive to expressing feelings and opinions, the ability to teach without imposing one's own values on students, effective communication skills, genuine warmth, empathy, openness, concern, and respect for others, good rapport and enjoyment of students, respect for all individuals regardless of individual differences, and a sense of humor (Cook, Kirby, Wilson, and Alter, 1984). The list seems endless! As Michael Carrera, a well-known sex educator, has noted, teachers of human sexuality have to be super teachers (Carrera, 1981).

CONCLUSION

The workshop experience and views of a small group of Greek American professionals reveal the dire need for addressing the issue of sex education in the Greek American Community. The extent to which other Greek Americans think and feel similarly is an empirical question. Further, there is a need for research on the sexual attitudes and behaviors of Greek American youth, and the influence of the Greek American family regarding issues of sexuality.

A consistent message that conscientious and concerned individuals who have developed quality programs in the United States convey is that programs be designed according to the needs and values of individual communities. This involves input from a variety of community leaders who are well-respected and concerned with the problems of young people. Parents, as one key source, have been identified earlier. Other people include key school administrators, members of the school board, students, teachers, school nurses, counselors, physicians, clergy, and local political leaders. The participation of these individuals is a means for assuring support and implementation of a well designed program.

Ultimately, the aim of a sex education program in the school setting is to empower parents. The program is a catalyst for that empowerment. A quality sex education program is consistent in design and content with Greek American values in this respect. It acts to buffer the negative impact of modern culture on a priority of Greek life, that of family. At the same time, it provides new roles for Greek American youth that are centered in equality of the genders, roles which I see as positive aspects of modernization. For these reasons, it seems to me that this is a most appropriate and critical time for the Greek American community to consider designing and implementing a quality sex education program in the Greek American school system.

REFERENCES

Carrera, M. (1981). *Sex: The facts, the acts and your feelings.* New York: Crown Publishers.

Carrera, M., & Caldrerone M. (1980). The SIECUS/NYU principles basic to education for sexuality. *Sexual Information and Education Council of the United States Report, 8,* 3-10.

Cook, A. T., Kirby, Wilson, & Alter. (1984). *Sexuality Education: A Guide to Developing and Implementing Programs.* Santa Cruz: Network Publications.

Dickman, I. R. (1984). *Winning the Battle for Sex Education.* New York: Sex Information and Education Council of the United States.

New York City Board of Education. (1985). *Grades K through 12 Family Living Including Sex Education.* Office of Curriculum Development and Support, Division of Curriculum and Instruction, New York, New York.

Orfanos, S. D., & Psomiades, H. J. (Co-chairs). (1986, May). Conference on Education and Greek Americans: Process and Prospects. New York.

Planned Parenthood of Northern New England. (1983). *K-12 Family Life Education Curriculum: Vols. 1 and 2.* Burlington, Vermont: Planned Parenthood of Northern New England.

Strong, B., & Reynolds, R. (1982). *Understanding Our Sexuality.* St. Paul, Minnesota: West Publishing Company.

CHAPTER 11

A NEEDS ASSESSMENT OF GREEK AMERICAN SCHOOLS IN NEW YORK CITY

SPYROS D. ORFANOS AND SAM J. TSEMBERIS

The history of Greek American schools is long, while the study of Greek American schools is relatively short. The first Greek parochial school was established in Chicago in 1908 (Lagios, 1976). For many Greek Americans the socialization experiences of the parochial school are second only to those of the family.

The importance of education for Greeks in maintaining and transmitting Greek culture has been articulated in the English language writings of Farmadakis (1981), Nikolopoulou (1986), Panayiotou (1979), and Scourby (1984). Kopan (1978) and Moskos (1980) noted the value attributed to the educated person in Greece, and Scourby (1984) commented on the high social status of education. The importance placed on education is also evident in the study on occupational stereotyping in American and Greek cultures conducted by Malikiosi (1976). He found Greeks perceived educators more positively than did Americans, while Americans perceived health professionals more favorably than did Greeks. Hines (1973) studied achievement motivation in Greeks, Greek Americans, Greek New Zealanders, and non-Greeks in the United States and New Zealand. The Greek group showed significantly higher achievement motivation scores across generations and cultures. Majoribanks (1984) interviewed 120 Greek families in Australia in which Greek was the primary language and found that compared to Anglo Australians and Southern Italian Australians, Greek Australian adolescents were characterized by higher educational and occupational aspirations. The study also found that the Greek Australian adolescents, more so than the other groups, perceived their parents as expressing much encouragement and showing an interest in their schooling. While caution is indicated in making inferences from studies conducted in other countries (Huberman, 1987), the fit between the Australian data and anecdotal American impressions is good (Saloutos, 1980).

Many Greek Americans have experienced either day schools, afternoon schools, Sundays schools, public school bilingual classes, or to a lesser extent theological seminaries. Saloutos (1980) discussing community life in the early Greek American settlements writes:

> As the first American-born generation began to make its appearance, so did the Greek-language school. These schools were often an adjunct to the parish church and were a means both of maintaining communication between parent and child and of preserving the Greek heritage in the new land . . . Classes usually were held in an improvised classroom in a church basement, rented hall, or vacant store after public-school day had ended.

> As a rule the Greek parish priest did the teaching, sometimes he had been the classroom teacher in his native village or town. His educational training was probably limited, however, and his new teaching assignment could be a burdensome chore. Learning was by rote, the disciplinary methods stern, and the climate for learning stultifying. (p. 433)

From their inception the Greek American schools had an interdependent relationship with the local parish and a perfunctory relationship with the varied representatives of the Archdiocese. In 1931, Archbishop Athenagoras, consistent with his policy of centralization, recognized the need for a uniformity among the schools. He founded the Supreme Educational Council. With the increase in immigration, by 1935 there were 414 afternoon schools and five day schools in America (Lagios, 1976; Scourby, 1984). In an article cited by Lagios and appearing in the *Orthodox Observer* in 1935, Stephanopoulos reported that the Greek schools needed funds and supervisors so that the following objectives could be accomplished:

1. Operate the schools and develop a uniform system of teaching in them.
2. Develop a standard curriculum.
3. Create student interest and more respect for the teachers.
4. Provide a coordinated teaching staff with proper supervision so as to establish a more effective seminar approach for teaching.
5. Praise and reward the teaching staff.
6. Offer social and economic independence for the teachers.
7. Develop more Greek schools in America.
8. Compile exact and detailed statistics which are needed in evaluating the schools (Lagios, 1976, p. 56).

The steady increase in the number of Greek American days schools was, in part, a result of the discriminatory education policies of the major cities in which Greek immigrants lived. Sarason and Doris (1979) describe the unfortunate fate that Italian immigrant children experienced during the early part of the century in the American public schools. Prejudice and a lack of English language skills caused many of these children to be systematically and nonempirically judged as intellectually deficient and placed in classes for the mentally retarded. A similar fate befell Greek immigrant children as their numbers in public schools increased after World War I (Kopan, 1981). With the continued influx of Greek immigrants, pressure was placed on local school boards, as early as the 1930s, for the teaching of Greek in public schools. Such proposals met with very limited success.

During the next three decades there were small increments in the number of Greek day schools consistent with the immigration patterns of those years. However, the patterns changed as a result of the Immigration Act of 1965 which spurred the entry of 86,344 Greeks into the United States from 1966 to 1971 (Scourby, 1984). This seemed to have an effect on public schools, and coupled with the pluralistic society and ethnic pride themes that were promulgated by educators in the 1960s helped to produce Greek bilingual programs in Chicago and New York, funded by federal grants from Title VII—The Bilingual Education Act of 1967 (Saloutos, 1980). Prior to this period, the options for parents interested in teaching their children the Greek language and culture were limited to the afternoon schools and the day schools.

For the academic years 1985-1986 the Department of Education (formerly the Supreme Education Council) of the Greek Orthodox Archdiocese of North and South America listed 406 afternoon schools and 23 day schools (Yearbook, 1986). The total enrollment in the fall of 1985 was 7,260 pupils. Of the day schools, eleven were in New York City, two in Chicago, seven in other parts of the United States, two in Canada, and one in South America. Two of the New York City schools offered high school programs. There were 3,381 (47% of the total enrollment) students reportedly enrolled in the eleven days schools in New York City. In a study of 160 first-, second-, and third-generation Greek Americans in the New York City Metropolitan area, Scourby (1980) found a significant decrease in Greek school attendance with each subsequent generation. Archdiocese statistical information, while sparse, supports this decreasing trend in enrollment.

Saloutos (1980) considered the quality of education in the schools and reported that "their effectiveness in teaching the Greek language varies considerably and most have trouble obtaining qualified teachers" (p. 439). The results of interviews with various educational leaders indicate that they believe there is a lack of information on the effectiveness and efficiency of the schools. This pertains to the teaching of the Greek language and to the basic subject areas, such as, language arts, reading and mathematics. A doctoral dissertation by George Lagios (1976), addressed the historical development of Greek American schools. He did not provide any data-based information on the education levels of those attending the schools. In addition, Lagios treated his subject with reverence rather than intellectual curiosity and perhaps this is why he failed to provide any information that may have been regarded as a criticism of the schools.

The present study sought to address issues pertaining to the strengths, deficits, and needs of the eleven Greek American day schools in New York City. It was conducted as a needs assessment. The term "needs assessment" was used as an organizational method of planned listening, data gathering, and reflective feedback (Lundquist, 1982). There are no previous empirical studies on this subject and yet several authors, dating back to 1935, have repeatedly called for this type of investigation. Also, given the current interest in educational accountability, it is important that we increase our understanding of the educational, administrative, and economic issues relevant to the Greek American day schools.

There are several limitations to this study. First, it does not examine actual behavior of students and teachers in the schools. Second, it does not study the needs articulated by students or parents. It relies on information provided by the educators and while that is a satisfactory starting point, it is not comprehensive. A third limitation concerns the complicated interactive nature of the subsystems under study. The Greek American day school is a subsystem of the educational culture, the Greek American culture, and the culture of the Greek Orthodox Church. The other larger systems are not studied here. Finally, Greek American day schools in New York City may be substantially different than those in other parts of the country. The results of the study are interpreted with these limitations in mind.

METHODOLOGY

Two questionnaires were used in this study: a semi-structured interview for the principals and a structured questionnaire for the teachers. The study was conducted in Spring 1986.

The principals' questionnaire consisted of 51 items concerning the school's organizational structure, principal's education, experience, budget and sources of funding, curriculum, instruction, evaluation programs, support services, policy formation, and their school's strengths and needs. The teacher questionnaire consisted of 31 items that assessed the nature of the teacher's duties, perception of school climate, a rank ordering of 13 specific needs that their school may have, and questions about their education and experience. Teachers were asked to place the numbers between 1 and 13 in order of importance next to items such as, "improve the student's basic skills performance," "develop a program for 'slow learners' and 'underachievers,'" "institute an inservice training program for teachers aimed at improving performance in the classroom," "improving the Greek language program," and "develop a program to educate children about drug and alcohol abuse." These needs items were modified versions of those developed by Shumk, Runkel, Arends, and Arends (1977).

The schools were located in the boroughs of Brooklyn, Manhattan, and Queens. Only the elementary schools were included. Initially, each school principal was contacted and informed about the study and all eleven agreed to participate. The principals were asked to place an envelope containing a cover letter, the teacher questionnaire, and a stamped addressed envelope in all their classroom teachers' mailboxes. Principals and teachers were guaranteed that their individual responses would be kept confidential and only general statistical results would be published. Of the 170 teachers in the eleven schools only 35 (21%) returned the envelope. All of the eleven principals completed their interview.

RESULTS

Principals' Report

The majority of the principals were born in the United States of Greek parents and had completed graduate degrees in education (see Table 1). They supervised an average of 15 teachers, two of whom were Greek teachers. The model school had about 265 students, 80% of which were born in the United States of Greek parents. Instruction was available from kindergarten to the eighth grade with an average of 21 students per class.

Most school buildings were an annex of, or attached to, the local church. They were built on average around 1961, with classrooms housed in renovated basements, auditoriums, and attics. The model school had an annual budget of $400,000 derived primarily from tuition and fund raising. Principals estimated that slightly more than five percent of the operating expenses were contributed by the host parish. The Archdiocese's Department of Education reported that the parishes contribute 25% to 30% of the annual school budgets (Yearbook, 1986).

TABLE 1
SELECTED BACKGROUND INFORMATION OF THE SCHOOLS AND PRINCIPALS

Selected Background Information	*N*	Range
Schools	11	
Average School Age	25	6-74
Average Budget/Year	$400,000	
Pupils	2926	
Range of Grades		
Kindergarten — 8	5	
Nursery — 8	4	
Kindergarten — 6	1	
Kindergarten — 9	1	
Average pupils per class	21	5-38
Principals	11[a]	
Years in position	4.8	1-17
Birthplace		
USA	7	
Greece	4	
Highest academic degree		
Masters	4	
Professional Degree	5	
Doctorate	2	
Teaching Staff		
Full-time	170[b]	
Part-time	19[c]	

[a]Technically, one of the interviewees was an assistant principal, but functionally an elementary school principal. Seven of the principals were male, and four were female.
[b]Thirty-six teachers or 21% of the full-time faculty teach Greek.
[c]This number consists of art, music, physical education and Greek

The organizational structures of the schools were typically hierachical with the principal on the top rung, and teachers and students each a step down the ladder. There was also an assistant principal in five of the schools. Eight of the principals described a collaborative decision-making process with the school board. The school boards usually consisted of the principal, members of a parents organization, and members of the parish council. The three schools not employing a collaborative process with the school board reported that relations with the board were "tense." The relation of the Archdiocese Board of Education to the schools was categorized as bureaucratic but not functional by ten of the eleven principals. Educational and administrative leadership was provided by the local schools and school boards and the Archdiocese was described as showing interest only in the Greek language and culture programs.

All the principals stated that their schools' goals were to provide students with basic knowledge of the major subject areas and to develop Greek American values. Curriculum and instruction was reported to follow the guidelines established by the New York State Department of Education for the major subject areas: language arts, reading, mathematics, science, and social studies. All schools devoted approximately 45 minutes of classroom instruction time per day to the teaching of Greek language and culture. The Greek language classes were conducted according to grade and age level except for two schools which employed a levels system based on the individual student's ability in the Greek language. Religion was usually taught by the parish priest on a once a week basis. Only one of the eleven schools provided instruction in sex education and drug and alcohol education. Programs were not available in any of the schools for assessment and instruction of children with handicaps or "gifted" children. Five of the schools received some support for disadvantaged children under Chapter 1 (or Title 1 of the Federal Elementary and Secondary Education Act). This provided limited part-time instruction in remedial reading, mathematics, and language (English as a Second Language) for those children living in economically depressed neighborhoods.

All schools used standardized tests to evaluate students' progress in reading and mathematics. Six different tests are used by the eleven schools making comparisons among the schools very difficult. Seven of the principals reported above average test scores for their students, and four reported average scores. Only three of the principals submitted actual test scores for analysis. The majority of the principals believed that the achievement test results were not valid due to problems with test construction and the use of standardization norms that were not developed for their culturally diverse population.

Principals identified three percent of their students as having learning and/or behavior problems requiring referral to special education programs for diagnosis and treatment. Across the schools, this was a total of 89 students. Four schools made ten referrals to the New York City Board of Education's Committee on the Handicapped (COH). Another ten children were referred to private practitioners or agencies. According to the principals, the remaining students (about 75%) were not referred due to the parent's fear that their child (and indirectly their family) would be stigmatized by such a referral. Limited community resources, that is, lack of adequate mental health and special education services sensitive to Greek Americans was offered as a second reason.

Principals' perceived their schools' strengths as follows:

1. The collaborative church-school relationship within the community provided support and agreement on educational goals.
2. The staff was judged to be highly professional and cohesive.
3. The small teacher-to-student ratios and the size of the schools made for a manageable setting.

The needs identified, and listed according to the priority they were given by the majority of principals, were the following:

1. To increase the number of faculty members because teachers were overworked.
2. Increasing teacher salaries was viewed as critical because experienced and competent teachers are constantly transferring to the much higher paying New York City Board of Education.
3. More classroom and office space was needed because school areas were extremely crowded.
4. The problem of declining enrollment needed to be solved.
5. There was a need to centralize across schools to facilitate the transfer of students from school to school, and to reduce operating expenses by purchasing supplies as a group (i.e. furniture, testing materials).

6. To hold ongoing planned meetings among all
principals in order to reduce their sense of isolation.

A number of principals expressed concern over parents' difficulty with distinguishing between achievement, ability and
effort. Parents believed that achievement is not a matter of
ability but due to effort. Further, concern was expressed
because many students held ethnocentric beliefs with pre-
judicial attitudes towards other ethnic and racial groups.
Principals also reported that between the ages of 10 and 13
a number of students began to cause behavioral disturbances
and seemed ashamed of their cultural heritage. The view was
also expressed that perhaps the students were often sheltered
and protected from the American cultural mainstream in
these Greek day schools.

Teachers' Report

Close to eighty-three percent of the teacher respondents
were female. Their mean age was 36 years, but the majority
were considerably younger. They had an average of nine years
teaching experience, and 51% had five years of experience
or less. The majority (60%) held a master's degree or above,
and had obtained at least one of their degrees in education
(74%). Sixteen teachers (46%) identified themselves as
Greek or Greek American, and the remainder indicated other
American ethnicity. Eighty-nine percent of the teachers identified English as their primary language. Only two of the
teachers participating in this study taught in Greek.

The teachers taught grade levels ranging from kindergarten to eighth grade. Sixteen teachers (46%) taught various grade levels, mostly in the upper levels (grades 5-8).
On the average, teachers had instructional contact with
silghtly over 60 students per year. Teachers identified a total
of 237 (12%) of their pupils as having learning and/or
behavior problems.

The majority of the teachers (83%) thought that their
contacts with students in the schools were, for the most part,
satisfying and rewarding. Over 85% of the teachers at least
partially agree with the statement, "The morale of the teachers in this school is high." The majority of teachers (60%)

TABLE 2
SELECTED BACKGROUND INFORMATION ON TEACHERS

Selected Background Information	N	Percentage
Age		
20 through 25	6	17.1
26 through 30	9	25.7
31 through 35	6	17.1
36 through 40	4	11.4
41 through 45	2	5.7
46 through 50	2	5.7
51 through 55	3	8.6
56 through 60	1	2.9
60 +	1	2.9
Missing	1	2.9
Sex		
Male	6	17.1
Female	29	82.9
Ethnicity		
Greek	10	28.6
Greek American	6	17.1
Other American	18	51.4
Missing	1	2.9
Education		
Bachelor's	14	40.0
Master's	18	51.4
Master's +	3	8.6
Years of Teaching Experience		
1-3	11	31.4
4-7	7	20.0
8-11	8	22.9
12-15	3	8.6
16-19	2	5.7
20 +	4	11.4

Note. N = 35.

would agree to choose teaching as a career if they could plan it again. Finally, 92% of the teachers at least partially agree that their schools made effective use of the individual teacher's ability and talent.

Teachers' ranked ordered perceptions of their schools' major needs are presented in Table 3. In order of priority, teachers ranked the need for developing a program for "slow learners" and "underachievers," as the most important need facing their schools. Improving performance on basic skills was ranked second, and increasing motivation and desire for learning was third. Developing a substance abuse educational program, instituting a program for teacher communication skills training, and improving the Greek language program were ranked as the three lowest priority needs.

TABLE 3
TEACHER'S RANK ORDERING OF MOST IMPORTANT SCHOOL NEEDS

Rank	Need
1	Develop a program for "slow learners" and "underachievers."
2	Improve the student's performance on basic skills.
3	Increase the children's motivation and desire to learn.
4	Improve the discipline and behavior of "difficult" children.
5	Developing an enrichment program.
6	Improve the parent's involvement in the children's education.
7	Institute an in-service training program for teachers aimed at improving their classroom performance.
8	Improve children's adherence to moral, religious and ethical standards.
9	Develop a health education and sex education program.
10	Develop an effective computer literacy program.
11	Develop a program to educate children about drug and alcohol abuse.
12	Institute a training program for teachers aimed at improving interpersonal relations and communication skills.
13	Improve the Greek language program.

DISCUSSION

The philosophies of the eleven schools were remarkably similar and focused on the teaching of basic academic skills and Greek American values. The importance on the former is underlined by the second place need ranking it was given by the teachers. Since improving students' basic skills was considered a major need by the teachers and it was the principals' first goal, this may indicate a serious perceived deficiency in this area. It may also reflect the current educational

Zeitgeist which emphasizes "getting back to basics." The second goal of the principals' philosophy, fostering Greek American values, indicates that these schools are not geared towards producing Greeks, but to providing for the development of "American citizens with pride in their Hellenic heritage." Given the isolation reportedly experienced by the principals, the fact that they held a common philosophy is noteworthy. It may reflect the consistency of the goals and needs of each community to provide education, culture, and language to its constituents. It is after all, the local communities that hire the principals and priests which serve on the local school boards.

An integral part of any school curriculum is the assessment of pupil performance. Assessment services in the Greek American day schools are limited to teacher developed tests and the administration of standardized achievement tests. Since these schools used six standardized testing programs, it is difficult to compare scores. All major school boards in New York State use only one standardized testing program within a district. We cannot compare the Greek schools to each other or with the New York City public schools without the use of one standardized test and public disclosure of summary scores. This has many important implications. For example, a parent deciding on what Greek school to enroll his or her child cannot make an informed decision about the academic level of that school. Just as important, the schools reduce the probability of accurately placing a transfer student from one day school to another. Furthermore, they cannot monitor their curriculum in order to maintain successful programs and modify deficient ones in a way that would better prepare their students to do well when they inevitably enter American high schools or colleges. On the other hand, the reservations that some principals have about the standardized testing programs may not be such a shortcoming given the phenomena of over-reliance on norm-referenced measures that have saddled education practice (Keith, 1987). The point is that testing programs can be beneficial only if they are used intelligently and sensitively.

The evaluation of the Greek language programs is relatively better. Eight of the eleven day schools reported that 95% of their graduating pupils (usually eighth graders) passed the New York State Regents Examination in Greek. It should be noted, however, that the Regents Foreign Languages Examinations typically require only three years of language instruction.

Estimates across the country of the number of children needing special educational and mental health services because of learning and/or behavioral problems range from 10% to 25% (Fishman, Torres, & Silver, 1984; Neeper & Lahey, 1983). Teachers need to know if the children they are working with have specific learning and/or emotional handicaps. Prior to Public Law 94-142, the law mandating free and appropriate education for all children with handicapping conditions, this had been a marginal interest in public schools, and it remains even less so in the parochial schools. There is a great discrepancy between the estimate of 3% of the children needing special services given by the principals and the estimate of 12% given by the teachers. This is probably due to the different access each has to the students and thus to the resulting difference in their perceptions. Other studies have found that teachers have a tendency to be sensitive to the prevalence of learning and behavioral difficulties of their students (Lambert, 1976). The teachers in this study ranked as their schools' most important need the development of a program for "slow learners" and "underachievers." Historically, slow learners and underachievers have been among the most difficult group of students for teachers to work with (Sarason, 1982).

A student who reads poorly in a Greek American school could be doing so because of any number of reasons: she or he is not taught properly, there is a cognitive impairment, receptive language difficulty compounded by the teaching of a second language, motivation is low, there are serious family problems, or other psychoeducational issues. Assessment of such problems and more importantly the interventions to treat them can only be determined by guidance counselors, psychologists, or other related personnel. In general, the Greek American schools do not have such personnel or the mechanisms for making such referrals. On very rare occasions, psychoeducational and speech and language assessments may be referred to Chapter 1 personnel or to the Committees on the Handicapped. In some instances, referrals have been made to community mental health centers. However, the waiting lists at these centers are long and the services are not oriented towards psychoeducational assessments. Given the importance for the early identification of children with special needs the lack of such service is critical. Christopoulos (1986) studied the referral patterns to a community mental health center servicing Greek American and other ethnic families (Hellenic American Neighborhood Action Committee's Child and Family Counseling Service) and found that Greek American children were referred for assistance at approximately age ten, while children of other ethnic groups with similar problems were referred at age eight, that is significantly earlier, for assistance. These findings coincide with the principals' observations that at the age of about ten, students began to experience behavioral and social difficulties. It also addresses the parental issues regarding the stigma of such a referral and the parents' willingness to give increased effort every chance to alter achievement before they consider that it may really be a matter of ability, or in these cases, a lack of it.

Adherence to traditional curricula and to the New York State guidelines were reported by the principals. Students with superior intellectual capacities were probably not being adequately served in the day schools. Despite an explosion in the field of gifted children's education and research (Council for Exceptional Children, 1978), interest in enrichment programs was ranked fifth by the teachers. Perhaps this is because of the common misconceptieon that gifted children will survive without clearly differentiated programs (DeMars, 1984). Health and sex education and substance abuse education programs were ranked even lower in importance by teachers in relation to the other items in this needs assessment. Furthermore, these instructional services are practically non-existent in the Greek American schools. This may appear surprising given the emphasis such programs are given in the public schools and other parochial schools. There has even been an increase in the implementation of such educational programs across the country (Wagner & Hawk, 1984), yet the Greek American schools have not followed suit. The reasons for this may be due to the taboo, denial, and misconceptions with which these subjects are viewed by Greek Americans (see Lefkarites in Chapter 10).

The major needs identified by principals in this study have to do with personnel and physical plant resources. Principals expressed the need for more and better paid faculty. Parochial schools generally have reputations for higher academic standards and fewer discipline problems than public schools since they can choose their students (Wolfle, 1987). This has been used as a recruiting devise by some schools, but more than this will be needed given the present salaries offered in the public sector. In a study of 102 Colorado schools, Turner, Camilli, Kroc, and Hoover (1986) used a sophisticated methodological design and analysis and found that salary incentives offered to teachers influence student achievement. The proposed Archdiocese salary scale for teachers with a Master's degree plus 30 graduate credits and 14 years of experience is $21,500 (Greek Orthodox Archdiocese of North and South America, 1985). In the New York City public schools a teacher with similar education and experience earns above $35,000 (Big Raises, 1987). It should be noted that the local school boards only take the Archdioceses salary proposal under advisement and can, and usually do act independently. Teacher salaries are closely tied to tuition and fundraising.

Principals, like teachers, are in lonely professions despite being in densely populated environments. They are required to give of themselves both intellectually and emotionally. Many of the principals in this study expressed a need for regular group contact with each other to counteract the isolation they were experiencing. Bringing the principals together in problem-solving groups may increase their ability to deal more effectively with educational matters. The needs and problems they experience do not reside in them as individuals but are an outgrowth of the schools and school system that is their responsibility (Sarason, 1982). The majority of principals expressed a strong desire for centralization across the schools, some even suggested that the Archdiocese act as the centralizing agent. Others strongly opposed this, preferring solely an educationally-based agenda for such meetings. Principals' meetings would permit the purchasing of materials in bulk, and provide the opportunity for sharing educational ideas, and finding creative ways to cope with limited resources.

There was no indication that the Archdiocese has the inclination or the economic and educational leadership necessary to engage in a centralization of the Greek American day schools. This contradicts a widely held public belief that the schools in large measure are run by the Archdiocese. The schools can be viewed as independent systems that resemble the Ancient Greek city-states. The eleven schools are mainly controlled by their respective communities.

The nature of the relationships the Greek American day schools have with outside agencies and groups appears to be

similar to the ingroups and outgroups that Triandis discusses
in Chapter 2 in this book. The teachers participating
in this study were satisfied with their work and believed to
be valued. Indeed, the principals stated that their staffs were
of high caliber and that they had close interpersonal relationships with them. Further, the majority of the principals
reported good working relationships with their community
school boards. In Triandis' framework, the school personnel
and community board members are an ingroup. That is,
ingroup members show trust, support, and cooperation toward
each other, and are guarded towards outgroup members. Outgroup members in the case of the Greek American schools may
be private or public service agencies, such as the Archdiocese,
Committees on the Handicapped, or researchers conducting
a needs assessment of the schools. Triandis, however, warns
that ingroups can become insulated and self-defeating.

Finally, the Greek American schools must begin to view
themselves as part of the larger social system and actively
establish working relationships with each other and with a
variety of outside agencies. This needs assessment gives every
indication that the Greek American schools are struggling
with many of the same issues that other public and parochial
schools are facing, namely, limited resources, two cultures,
"the system," and a desire for leadership. Historians of education, as well as those of Greek Americans, will find much that
is familiar in this exploratory study. It is necessary to continue and to expand the research on the Greek American day
schools. There is a need to better understand the achievement
and motivational levels of the children in these schools and
their relationships to their Greek and American worlds. There
is a need to know what solutions have helped the children,
their families, and the schools, and what issues continue to
create problems. It is hoped that more research will be conducted so that we can better understand how the day schools
can better serve the children and parents of the Greek American community.

REFERENCES

Big raises agreed on for Rochester teachers. (1987, August 23). *The New York Times*, p. 43.

Christopoulos, A. (1986, May). Mental health services for Greek American school children. Paper presented at the conference on Education and Greek Americans: Process and prospects. New York.

Council of Exceptional Children. (1978). *The nation's commitment to the education of gifted and talented children and youth: Summary and findings from a survey of states.* Reston, VA.: The Council of Exceptional Children.

DeMers, S. T. (1984). Designing programs for the gifted and talented. In C. A. Maher, R. J. Illback, & J. E. Zins (Eds.), *Organizational psychology in the schools: A handbook for professionals* (pp. 198-210). Springfield, Ill.: Charles C Thomas.

Fishman, M. E., Torres, L. B., & Silver, L. B. (1984). *NIMH announcement of support for child and adolescent mental health research and research training.* Rockville, MD: National Institute of Mental Health.

Frangoudakis, A. (Ed.). (1981). Education in Greere today: A symposium [Special issue]. *Journal of the Hellenic Diaspora, 11* (1-2).

Greek Orthodox Archdiocese of North and South America. (1985). *Revised salary scale, June 1985.* New York: Greek Orthodox Archdiocese of North and South America.

Hines, G. H. (1973). The persistence of Greek achievement motivation across time and culture. *International Journal of Psychology, 8,* 285-288.

Huberman, M. (1987). How well does educational research really travel? *Educational Researcher, 16,* 5-13.

Keith, T. Z. (1987). Assessment research: An assessment and recommended interventions. *School Psychology Review, 16,* 276-289.

Kopan, A. T. (1978, February). Greek ethnicity and American education. *Greek World,* pp. 24-25.

Kopan, A. T. (1981). Greek survival in Chicago: The role of ethnic education, 1890-1980. In P. d'A Jones & M. G. Holli (Eds.), *Ethnic Chicago* (pp. 86-125). Grand Rapids, Mich.: William B. Eerdman's.

Lagios, G. A. (1977). *The development of Greek American education in the United States: 1908-1973 its theory, curriculum, and practice.* Unpublished doctroal dissertation, University of Connecticut. (University Microfilms No. 77-16, 718).

Lambert, N. M. (1976). Children's problems and classroom interventions from the perspective of classroom teachers. *Professional Psychology, 7,* 507-517.

Lundquist, G. W. (1982). Needs assessment in organizational development. In C. R. Reynolds & T. B. Gutkin (Eds.), *The handbook of school psychology* (pp. 936-968). New York: Wiley.

Malikiosi, M. X. (1976). Occupational stereotyping in American and Greek cultures. *Journal of Social Psychology, 99,* 13-19.

Marjoribanks, K. (1984). Ethnicity, family environment and adolescents' aspirations: A follow-up study. *Journal of Educational Research, 77,* 166-171.

Moskos, C. C. (1980). *Greek Americans: Struggle and success.* Englewood Cliffs, NJ: Princeton.
Neeper, R., & Lahey, B. B. (1983). Learning disabilities of children. In C. E. Walker & M. C. Roberts (Eds.), *Handbook of clinical child psychology* (pp. 680-696). New York: Wiley.
Nikolopoulou, A. (1986). School psychology in Greece. *Journal of School Psychology, 24,* 325-333.
Panayiotou, M. A. (1979). Psychology within the educational system of Greece. In C. D. Catterall (Ed.), *Psychology in the schools in international perspective: Vol. 3* (pp. 86-102). Columbus, OH: International School Psychology Steering Committee.
Saloutos, T. (1980). Greeks. In S. Thernstrom (Ed.), *Harvard Encyclopedia of American Ethnic Groups* (pp. 430-440). Cambridge, Mass.: Harvard University.
Sarason, S. B., & Doris, J. (1979). *Educationally handicapped, public policy, and social history: A broadened perspective on mental retardation.* New York: Free Press.
Sarason, S. B. (1982). *The culture of the school and the problem of change* (2nd ed.). Boston: Allyn and Bacon.
Scourby, A. (1984). *The Greek Americans.* Boston: Twayne.
Schmuck, R. A., Runkel, P. J., Arends, J. H., & Arends, R. I. (1977). *The second handbook of organizational development in schools.* Palo Alto, CA: Mayfield.
Turner, R., Camilli, G., Kroc, R., & Hoover, J. (1986). Policy strategies, teacher salary incentive, and student achievement: An explanatory model. *Educational Researcher, 15,* 5-11.
Wagner, D. I., & Hawk, D. E. (1984). Promoting health in schools. In C. A. Maher, R. J. Illback, & J. E. Zins (Eds.), *Organizational psychology in the schools: A handbook for professionals* (pp. 243-261). Springfield, Ill.: Charles C Thomas.
Wolfe, L. M. (1987). Enduring cognitive effects of public and private schools. *Educational Researcher, 16,* 5-11.
Yearbook. (1986). New York: Greek Orthodox Archdiocese of North and South America.

AUTHOR INDEX

SUBJECT INDEX

Achievement: 29, 94, 106; motivation, 185-186, 201; parental influence, 105, 111-115, 165-166
Action for Excellence, 11, *14*
Adult education, 13
American Hellenic Educational Progressive Association (AHEPA), 97, 100
A Nation at Risk, 11, *14*
Aspira vs. the Board of Education of the City of New York, 77, 152, *166*
Assessment: language tests, 151; of minority children, 152; in parochial schools, 192, 197
Assimilation, 91

Bilingual Education Act of 1968, 76
Bilingual education: additive bilingualism, 79; Basic Interpersonal Communication Skills (BICS), 78, 83; Cognitive/Academic Language Proficiency (CALP), 78; and community control, 74-75; and the Department of Education, Greek Orthodox Archdiocese, 82; differences in parochial and public schools, 75; Limited English Proficiency (LEP), 73, 87; misconceptions of in public schools, 77-81; and parental involvement, 86; and parochial schools, 82-84; politics of, 76-77, 88; and self-concept, 84; types of programs 73, 76-77, 84-85, 137, 148

California Achievement Test (CAT), 137
Carnegie Forum, 11, *14*
Center for Byzantine and Modern Greek Studies, Queens College of the City University of New York, 39
Children's Embedded Figures Test (CEFT), 139, 141
Civil Rights Act of 1964, 76, 151
Community School District 30, 79, 87
Council for Exceptional Children, 199
Cross-cultural psychology. *See* Research, social science
Cultural transmission, 12

Decision-making, 14
Department of Education, Greek Orthodox Archdiocese of North and South America, 82, *89*

NOTES ON CONTRIBUTORS

EVELYN P. ALTENBERG received her doctorate in linguistics from the Graduate Center of the City University of New York (CUNY) in 1981. The study on bilingual orthography perception was conducted while she was an Assistant Professor of Linguistics at Queens College of CUNY, where she currently maintains an affiliation. Her research interests include bilingual language processing, second language acquisition, and language attrition, and her articles have appeared in *Language Learning* and the *Journal of Verbal Learning and Verbal Behavior.*

JAMES R. CAMPBELL is an Associate Professor of Education at St. John's University. He is currently involved in several international studies including a national study of Greek children and a parallel study of Greek American children. The focus of these studies involves parental influence and the gender stereotypes that have been developed in the different cultures.

CHARLENE CONNOLY received her doctroal degree from St. John's University in 1985. She was a co-investigator in several studies involving gifted male and female high school students. She is currently Director of Health Education for Kaiser Permanente in California.

CHRYSIE M. COSTANTAKOS is a Professor of Child and Family Studies at Brooklyn College of the City University of New York (CUNY). She holds a B.A. in chemistry from Barnard Colleg, a M.S. in nutrition and an Ed.D. in marriage and families from Teachers College, Columbia University. She holds a certificate in gerontology from the Brookdale Center on Aging, Hunter College, CUNY, and is studying towards a certificate in family therapy at the Downstate Medical Center of the State University of New York. She is a past Chair and current member of the Greek American Behavioral Sciences Institute's Executive Board. She has numerous publications on Greek American studies, aging, nutrition, and consumer education.

MARY P. LEFKARITES received a B.S. in education from City College of the City University of New York (CUNY) in 1963, a M.S. in education from Hunter College, CUNY in 1967, and a Ph.D. from New York University in international community health education. Currently, she teaches at Hunter College, CUNY in the Women's Studies Program and the Department of Health and Physical Education in which she is Coordinator of School Health Education. In 1986, she was the recipient of the Pauli Murray Faculty Development Award at Hunter College, CUNY. She is the present Chair of the Greek American Behavioral Sciences Institute. Her present research focus is on health attitudes and practices of Greek Americans.

ARISTOTLE MICHOPOULOS is Associate Director of the Center for Greek Studies at the University of Florida. He received his B.A. in literature from the University of Athens, his M.A. in comparative literature from the Graduate Center of the City University of New York, and his Ph.D. from Florida State University. He is author of Γιά Μιά Νέα Δελφική 'Ιδέα, the "Kotylion Language Dominance Test," and various articles and papers ranging from educational testing, to comparative literature, education, humor, politics and poetry. He is currently working on a book tentatively titled: *Plato's Republic through computers.*

SPYROS D. ORFANOS is a psychologist in the special services program of the Board of Cooperative Educational Services of Rockland County. He engages in psychotherapy, consultation, and research. He received a Ph.D. in psychology from New York University (1986). He teaches educational psychology at Baruch College of the City University of New York (CUNY), clinical techniques at Fordham University's doctoral program in school psychology, and lectures on Greek American community issues at the Center for Byzantine and Modern Greek Studies of Queens College, CUNY. He has been a clinical instructor at New York University and the Downstate Medical Center of the State University of New York. A past Chair and current member of the Executive Board of the Greek American Behavioral Sciences Institute, he is also the research member of the Education Study Group of the American Orthopsychiatric Association, and is involved in research on training and education for the American Psychological Association's Division of School Psychology. He is preparing (with Sam J. Tsemberis) a collection of studies on the psychology of Greek Americans.

HARRY J. PSOMIADES received his early education at the Boston Public Latin School. He received his B.A. from Boston University and graduate training at Columbia University (M.I.A., Ph.D.). Before joining the faculty at Queens College of the City University of New York in 1965, he was Associate Dean of Columbia University's Graduate School of International Affairs. Currently he is Professor of Political Science and Director of The Center for Byzantine and Modern Greek Studies at Queens College. He has written extensively on the politics of the eastern Mediterranean, contributing over 100 articles in various books and professional journals. He is the author of *The Eastern Question: The Last Phase, A Study in Greek-Turkish Diplomacy* (1968), co-author of *Foreign Interference in Greek Politics: A Historical Perspective* (1976), co-editor of *The Greek American Community in Transition* (1982) and *The Teaching of Modern Greek in the English-Speaking World* (1984). In 1985, he was awarded an honorary Doctor of Letters degree (Litt. D.) by Hellenic College/Holy Cross Greek Orthodox School of Theology for his long and distinguished service to the Greek American community and to Greek letters.

MARY TERESA RYAN completed the study of bilingual orthography perception while a graduate student at Queens College of the City University of New York (CUNY). She was affiliated with LaGuardia Community College of CUNY. Currently, she is associated with a major New York publishing house. Her current research interests include other issues in orthography perception and comparative syntax.

JOHN SPIRIDAKIS holds a B.A. in English from the State University of New York, Stony Brook (1971), and an M.S. and Ph.D. from Florida State University in education. He has been Coordinator of the Bilingual Education Program at St. John's University since 1978. A former curriculum specialist with the New York City Board of Education, he developed Greek bilingual curricula and literature for the early grades. Currently, he serves on the Education Committee of the Greek Orthodox Archdiocese and the New York City Board of Education Chancellor's Commission on Bilingual Education. He is also a member of the Executive Board of the Greek American Behavioral Sciences Institute. His research and written work are largely in the areas of second language learning, cultural attitudes, learning styles, and self-concept.

LAWRENCE SVRCEK is currently completing his doctorate at St. John's University. His research involves a national study of elementary school children's home and school learning environments. He also serves as Vice-Principal of the Jamaica Day School of the St. Demetrios Greek Orthodox Church.

TERRY TCHACONAS holds a B.A. in psychology, an M.A. in political science, and an M.A. in the teaching of reading from City College of the City University of New York. He also holds a professional diploma in educational administration and supervision from Pace University. He was granted an Ed.D. from Columbia University in 1985 in the teaching of English as a second language. He is currently a public elementary school Assistant Principal and an Adjunct Assistant Professor at St. John's University. He has published several articles dealing with bilingual education, ethnic studies, and reading.

HARRY C. TRIANDIS is Professor of Psychology at the University of Illinois, Urbana-Champaign. His degrees are from McGill University in Montreal, the University of Toronto, and Cornell University (Ph.D., 1958). He is the author of *Attitude and Attitude Change* (1971), *The Analysis of Subjective Culture* (1972), *Variations in Black and White Perceptions of the Social Environment* (1976), *Interpersonal Behavior* (1977), and about 200 articles and chapters published in the standard psychological literature. He is Editor of the six-volume *Handbook of Cross-Cultural Psychology.* He is Past President of the International Association of Cross-Cultural Psychology, the Society for Personality and Social Psychology of the American Psychological Association, the Society for the Psychological Study of Social Issues, the Interamerican Society of Psychology (North and South America), and Past Chairman of the Society for Experimental Social Psychology.

SAM J. TSEMBERIS is Director of Research at the Division of Child and
Adolescent Psychiatry of the Downstate Medical Center of the State
University of New York. He received a Ph.D. in psychology from
New York University (1985). He teaches and supervises family
therapy at the School of Medicine at New York University's Medi-
cal Center and at the Hellenic American Neighborhood Action Com-
mittee's Child and Family Counselling Center. He is a past Chair
and a current member of the Greek American Behavioral Science
Institute's Executive Board. He is currently conducting research in
clinical and community psychology, and is co-editing (with Spyros
D. Orfanos) a collection of studies on the psychology of Greek
Americans.